Fearfully and Wonderfully Made:

My Journey to Self-Worth

By

Sandra Jackson (Griggs)

"I will praise you because I am fearfully and wonderfully made; wonderful are your works! My soul knows it well."

Psalm 139:14

Introduction

This is my story. It is written from my own personal memories, experiences and perspectives. It is not in any particular sequence so there may be some inconsistencies with the time frames for some events but everything written here happened to me. It is in no way meant to offend, hurt or demean any member of my family, nor people who have been a part of my life. It is just my testimony. As I often pondered the many aspects of my life, I realized that my testimony could help someone else who may have similar experiences as mine. I didn't think about it that way while I was going through some of the trials, but God inspired me to write about them so that I could encourage someone else. My love for writing and reading grew out of growing up being surrounded by books. My mother instilled in us the importance of having your own personal library. I began to have the idea of writing books about things that I thought were important to me many years ago and started two books. I started, stopped and then started again but then my computer crashed and I didn't have the foresight to put them onto a thumb drive (it may have not been available at that time, so thank God technology has advanced because now I use one!).

At the time, I had not yet decided to tell my story. I was focused on writing what I wanted to write about. God kept whispering to me that before I could finish those stories I had to write my own. I had been in spiritual bondage due to the physical, emotional and sexual abuse I had suffered throughout much of my life. Although outwardly I was able to function normally, inwardly, I was imprisoned. I was stuck. I had begun to believe the words that I constantly heard. I didn't value who I was, didn't think there was any beauty to me and didn't realize how much I had to offer. This story is graphic and raw in some places. As I peeled back layers of my life, I relived some of the most painful moments and was an emotional wreck while revisiting them. But I got through them. God allowed me to face my hurts to remove the fears that had consumed me for so much of my life. I want to help others who may have experienced those same hurts.

There are so many adults who have been molested as children and they are often found operating in cycles that have detrimental effects on every area of their lives. These spiral and often the abuse becomes generational. The saying goes, "hurt people hurt other people." This is often the case. They have bad relationships with their families, friends, neighbors, their co-workers and for most they end up with various addictions to drugs, food, porn, alcohol, shopping and a host of other things. Some of them become molesters themselves. But even if you have been molested as a child, there is hope for you to live free from the effects of that abuse and you can experience peace and joy. I am a living testament that you can be free.

Today, I am free. The completion of my story is the final shackle being removed so that I can continue to use the gifts that God has given me. This is just the beginning. My story is not over and there definitely is more for me to write but I had to remove the cork of pain that blocked the flow of the Spirit of God in my heart to be able to pour out what He has given me. As you read this story, my prayer is that you are encouraged to keep pushing forward. Even if you feel hopeless, worthless, weak, insignificant, defeated, irrelevant, just know that in God, you are fearfully and wonderfully made.

Twenty years ago today, I found him dead, lying on his bedroom floor. I thought that moment was the worst time in my life. I thought that my life was basically over. I never thought that I would recover from that horrible moment. Little did I know that it was just the beginning for me. God chose that dark moment to prepare me to move to another level in my life, away from the dependency on others to a deep, abiding trust in Him and His purpose for my life. Where do I begin telling my story? That moment was definitely not the darkest moment in my life. I've had other moments that were just as dark. It's funny though, as I thought about that day 20 years ago, I cried again. But those were not tears of sadness for a loss that I never thought I would experience, they were tears of joy for coming to the realization of how God used that moment to begin my journey to restoration. Just in that moment of reflection, He again showed me that His Sovereign plan takes precedent even in the face of difficult circumstances. On the day I found my grandfather dead in his room while I was alone in the house with my 5 small children, I had no idea that I would one day end up far away from the city I grew up in, living in a place that is the total opposite of the environment I had become accustomed to all my life. And this is the story of how I ended up living with my grandfather before he died, how I woke up to find him there and how God strengthened me to be able to stand today whole and renewed. Today, I realize that I am fearfully and wonderfully made.

I was born during the 1967 riots in Newark, NJ. I don't remember what was going on of course, but I remember hearing the story about how my mother or grandmother had been out to get me some milk when everything broke out. I am the oldest child and grandchild in my mother's family. My mother had me at age 17. She herself was born when my grandmother was between 16-18 years old. I am sure that I probably turned the house upside down with my arrival, but I guess everyone took to me when I was a baby. Our home was a 3 story house. The people that lived on the third floor were related to us. There was a family on the first floor at that time who were not related by blood but I played with the children often for my first years. I remember being around my aunts, uncle and cousins often, but they were older than me. I remember that I would sit around listening to them talk. I quickly became the center of attention. (At least I'd like to think so!) My aunts and uncle were my playmates! My uncle was my grandparent's only son and I loved spending time with him because my father wasn't around anymore a few years after I was born. I remember my uncle would play dress up with my dolls with me. He was very patient. I remember once while playing I told him I had to put on the doll's accessories and he was surprised that I knew that word! I was about 5, I think, but I remember him laughing and smiling when I told him that. My mother was the oldest child. The second floor apartment had two bedrooms, a spare room and a sun porch. For a few years before my youngest sister was born, we still lived there but then my mother moved us not too far from my grandparent's house into a garden apartment across town with a nice balcony sometime after my youngest sister's birth in 1975.

My mother had us at a young age but she always worked as far as I can remember. I believe she worked at night sometime during this period. I have one memory of her sitting with my next two sisters in the living room at my grandparent's house with her coat on and we were wearing pajamas. She must have been coming in or getting ready to go out to work but she took time to sit on the floor with us and let us play a game with all of her money. We were throwing it up in the air and she was helping us identify the coins. I remember laughing and playing with the money having a good old time. She was and still is a very intelligent woman. During my childhood, I remember her always stressing how important education was. We had tons of books. In fact, when the people on the first floor moved out and we moved back to the 3 story home on Custer, we had a wall in the entry of that apartment downstairs that she created a ceiling to floor library. We even took a picture in front of that wall. She encouraged us to read and I loved books. Another memory I have is one while we were still living on the second floor where she was in the bedroom that I guess was ours and I was in the front room. I was listening to records that were teaching the sound of the alphabet. I remember I was singing along with all of my heart. She was cheering me on while busy cleaning up the room. I also remember preschool. I attended a preschool located in a church down the street from our home, but my time there was difficult. I know I enjoyed painting and playing in the art center and with the toys. But there are memories during that time that are filled with fear and sadness. Even though I was surrounded by a loving family and had all of my needs met, there was a horrible spirit that had taken my family captive.

I have no idea when it began, but by the time it got to me, it had already destroyed several female family members. My family was large on both sides. There were always cousins, aunts and uncles visiting, so when either side came, the house was always full. My maternal great-grandparents had 5 children. My great-grandmother was from McColl, South Carolina. I don't know the whole story, but somehow, she ended up in Newark. She married my great-grandfather who worked for the railroad at one time. I didn't know a lot about them. We visited them often when I was young. My mother was close to her grandmother. She would take us to her house and we always had fun. But it was always a quiet, serene fun. My great-grandmother was a little lady with white hair from the time I can remember her. She was small and had a quiet voice but when she laughed, it would brighten up the room. Whenever we visited her, she had pound cake, vanilla bean ice cream or shortbread cookies for us. She would cook lamb and potatoes for dinner. We couldn't run or jump around her house because it was only a 3 room apartment. Her house always smelled of Dove soap. She used the pink kind. I still use it today and it reminds me so much of her.

The one profound difference at her house was that she had a stack of Daily Bread devotionals on her coffee table next to her huge family Bible. She had filled out the family members' names in the book. The book also had pictures of biblical scenes, like the Last Supper painted by Michelangelo, the temptation in the garden, Noah's Ark, and the Resurrection. I would look at that Bible all the time during our visits. Once when I was almost in my adolescent years, I remember my great-grandmother sitting with me talking about the stories in the Bible that I was reading. I know I asked her a lot of questions. I don't remember exactly what we talked about, but I remember having those conversations with her being so peaceful. Her answers to me about the Bible were so profound and I could feel her strong belief in them. She was a member of her church for as long as I knew her. She and my grandfather were stewards and served on boards. I don't know if her children went to church during their childhood, but just about every Easter Sunday growing up, I knew that our family was required to attend sunrise service. We would all get dressed early in the morning and we would go to the sunrise service and sit on the pew my great-grandmother reserved for us. She had a special seat and we all sat near her. After the services, we would go eat breakfast in the fellowship hall. My grandmother still sits on that pew!

My great-grandmother's church was the only opportunity I had as a child to hear about God. We weren't required to be in church every week. There were no Bibles lying around our home and there was no church music blaring from the radio. In fact, there was hardly any godly reference in our home. There was a lot of drinking, cussing and at times, weed smoking at home. My mother was militant about her culture. I grew up towards the end of the civil rights era when black power was becoming the battle cry for young African Americans. Our home was filled with things that represented our ethnicity. Yet while my mother promoted our culture, she also introduced us to other things. Along-side albums by Stevie Wonder, Marvin Gaye and Phoebe Snow, we had Mozart, Bach, Shubert and Tchykovsky. She enrolled us in ballet and violin classes and gave us bikes and skateboards to play with. My mother did the best she could to provide for us and give us opportunities to be successful. Her desire was for all four of us to go farther than she did. She was hard on us, but at the same time, she did her best to enrich our lives. She worked hard to make ends meet, but she was also involved in our school activities. She became our Girl Scout troop leader. We all were active in Girl Scouts. One year, as a troop leader, she was responsible for keeping a count of the cookies. So, we had huge cartons full of Girl Scout cookie boxes at our house. Well, leaving cookies in a house full of children is a recipe for disaster. I began sneaking into the cartons to eat cookies. Of course it started out small. I could hide a box somewhere undetectable, so I thought. I couldn't put the empty box in the trash, so I decided to hide it under my mattress. We had a sturdy bunk bed in our room and I slept on the top. A few boxes could be stashed and no one would be the wiser. Well of course, I started stealing more and hiding them under the mattress. I got away with it for a few weeks until one day, my mom came into our room and just so happened to lean her arm on the top of my bed. Now, she always came in our room. Sometimes she would lie on the bottom bunk and we would play and hang our heads down laughing with her and talking, having a good old time. But this particular day, she leaned on the top bunk and all she heard was "crinkle, crinkle". She said, "what the hell?" Low and behold, when she lifted the mattress, there was a mountain of empty cookie boxes there! She started yelling, and if my memory serves me correctly, I got a whooping, but I also remember her laughing about it later. Even today, whenever I think about it or talk about it, I crack up laughing!

There are a lot of good memories that I have of my childhood and many times, I did have happy experiences with my mother, sisters and other members of my family. But unfortunately, there are also some sad memories and there were times that I was not happy and neither was my mother. My grandmother and grandfather were teenage parents. I am not sure when they got married, but I do know that they both were barely out of high school. My grandparents brought the house on Custer

Avenue just after I was born in 1967. I believe it was in October, which would have made me four months old.

My grandfather had served in the Korean War. The story is that he altered his birth date so that he could enlist early. For a time, he lived with us in that house. I don't know when he moved out, but I have very few memories of him there. He had a green rocking chair in the front room that was his dinner chair. He would sit in front of that television with a tray with his dinner and a beer. I also have a few memories of riding in a car with him and my grandmother. I guess my mother and her siblings were there, but I recall once while riding in the front seat with no seatbelt on, he put me on his lap and let me drive. I think my grandmother was fussing, but I was having fun! I don't recall him doing a whole lot more than that. It seemed like all of a sudden he wasn't living with us. After that, I have a few memories of him standing out on the sidewalk talking to me, but not coming into the house. I recall times when he would drive up our block in the liquor truck that he drove for a living and stopped by. I didn't connect him with the word grandfather at that time, even though I knew he was my grandfather, because that is what they told me. I only remember my grandfather's parents vaguely. His mother died when I was very young. The only memory I have of her is my mother taking me to her apartment when she was sick. His father was around because my grandfather's sister lived on the third floor of the house we lived in. He was a little old man who had a bad stutter, but he was a sharp dresser and was well known around the neighborhood as "Sparky". He used to tell us that he was related to Frederick Douglas, but nobody knew for sure. We still don't know but maybe one day, we will look into it.

So I called these men "grandfather", but I didn't have a lot of grandfatherly affection for them. I found out later that my grandfather had other women and children in his life. I remember going with my mother to visit with him at some of these women's homes with their children. I even got close to some of them. But still he remained much of a stranger to me during those first years. By the time we went to live with him, I was fourteen. I thought he was a quiet man, but later, I began to think he was a mean man!

I don't know much about my father. I was told that he used to call me until I was about 5 years old. By then, he and my mother were not together. My sisters and I have different fathers, so I really had no concept of what a real father was either. Every few years, my mother would have a new man in her life. When we moved back to Custer Avenue on the first floor after my youngest sister was born, the man that was my baby sister's father was the only man that I could fit into that category, so for years I called him "Daddy". The other male figures in my life that did not fit into that category were my mother's only brother, my great uncles on both sides and the male cousins of my mother. They came to visit on occasion, but the only one that closely resembled a father was my uncle. In fact, I considered him my only father figure. When we lived on the second floor, he is the one who I spent considerable time with, talking, playing and listening to. When I was very young, he and my aunts became my playmates. I got along fine with them, but I was too young to realize what was happening to our family. I don't know exactly when, but by the time I came along, the damage had already been done and I soon became a victim of not one but two other predators.

By the time I started school, my mother had two more daughters. I was around four or five years old the first time I remember being molested. My mother would hang out with friends sometimes at night. I remember once when my mother was going out, she left me and my younger sister, who was probably between two and three years old, with a baby sitter at one of her friend's house. This young woman was supposed to be watching me, my sister and one or two other children that belonged to my mother's friends. There was a little boy who was younger than me there. I believe I was the oldest. The adults went out to party and left us with this young babysitter. I assume she was an older teenager. I recall we were in a bedroom and she was trying to make me and the boy or my sister and the boy perform sexual acts. I recall her taking a stick and hitting my sister on the legs because she kept crying. I then recall her taking me into a closet by myself where she laid me on the floor and sat her naked bottom on my face attempting to make me perform oral sex on her. I felt sickened and she kept hitting me with the stick. I don't know how long this lasted, but I remember my sister and the boy were still crying while this was going on and I guess eventually she had had enough and put us to bed.

I don't remember when my mom came to take us home, but I do remember a while later, maybe a few days, my mother, grandmother and some other relatives took me and my sister over to that house and there was a big commotion because my sister had bruises on her arms and legs. I don't remember what was said, but there was a lot of screaming and someone was pulling my sister's clothes up to show where she was bruised. I think I only had a few bruises on my arm, but they were showing the bruises on my sister's legs and thighs. I was very young but I wasn't crying though and I felt like I was all alone. I saw what was happening around me, but it felt as if I was not really there, just an observer. This became a coping mechanism for me throughout my entire life, as I began to withdraw from people and situations. Afterwards, I had begun acting out and having problems in preschool. In the beginning, I loved school. But after that incident, I didn't like going anymore. I remember I started coming to school in my pajamas because I would wet the bed at night. My mother was getting frustrated. She would spank me but I kept doing it. My first sister was born in October 1969 and my second sister was born in August of 1970. We lived on the second floor of 220 Custer Avenue with my grandparents, aunts and uncle for a period, but by the time my last sister was born in June 1975, I was in elementary school. I had been struggling with school because of what happened to me in preschool. I don't really remember much of those first years, except that my kindergarten teacher was my mother's teacher. She was nice to me and I liked her but I don't think I was doing well. I started becoming sexual at this time as I remember once that one of my aunts caught me under the covers with one of my sisters rubbing against each other with our pants down. I remember she yelled that she was going to tell my mother. Throughout the course of the next few years, I had begun to do the same thing to younger cousins and my youngest sister.

When a child is molested, it's like a switch has been turned on and they can't turn it off. Once they are introduced to sex it at a young age, everything becomes sexual for them. They may appear to be normal on the outside, but mentally they are seeking that gratification even though they don't fully understand it. If God does not step in and interrupt that mentality, most molested children will become molesters themselves. Although I started off heading down that path, God put His hand upon me before I could fall deeper into that abyss. I know that I have damaged family members that I love and I am truly sorry about the things that I have put them through, but I thank God for deliverance from that bondage. I look at where I am today and how I am able to teach children and have no desire to do anything to hurt them like that. I know that God has set me free! When my mother became pregnant with my youngest sister, we moved out of my grandparent's house into a garden apartment with my youngest sister's father across town. This man stayed with my mother for quite a few years. He had become my "Daddy". I loved him because he was always doing special things with me. He would take me to the store and buy me candy, chips and soda, which my mother never let me get. Even though he was only my baby sister's father, he always treated the rest of my sisters and I as if we were his own. I remember he would take me to this diner near our house and I would ride on his shoulders sometimes because I would get tired of walking and he would buy me pancakes for breakfast and tell the people that I was his daughter. Our apartment was nice and we had a balcony that my mother would sometimes set a blanket out on and we would have picnics for dinner there. I have some good memories of that apartment. I remember after my youngest sister was born, I would help my mom as she fed and bathed her. She would sit in the baby seat as we ate on the balcony. I even remember what I believe was one of the few Christmases we celebrated there. We had a tree that we decorated with blue ornaments. We all decorated the tree and put lights on the balcony. It was a fun time. But I had dark moments there too. I had been acting out in school since the incident with the baby sitter. There were also two boys that lived next door to us and I had a crush on one of them. I remember getting caught in between one of the walkways letting him feel me up and grind on me. After that, the other kids in the complex stopped playing with me. I still wasn't doing well in school either. I believe I was held back one year in school at one point during that time.

So along with the feelings of helplessness, loneliness and shame, I also struggled with worthlessness. I remember once while living in that apartment I was on punishment because of my math homework. I hated doing homework, especially math and my mother wouldn't let me come out of my room until I was finished. I had gotten a spanking after a while and she kept coming in to check and see if it was done. I was in that room for hours and she let me come out to eat dinner only to go right back to my room as my sisters were on the balcony having fun, watching television and playing. My "Daddy" was there and I remember them talking about me not doing my homework and misbehaving in school. He never disciplined me and I think that is why I began clinging to him. My mother told me once that my real father used to call me until I was about 5 years old. He would talk to me on the phone, making promises to come and see me but he never did. I must have taken his broken promises out on my mother because she told me that I used to tell her I hated her when I was little. I don't even remember talking to him but I know that by this time, I was really acting out.

Soon we moved back to Custer Avenue to the first floor. The family that lived there had moved out and we finally had enough room and lived right downstairs from Gramma. It was 6 rooms. At first I had my own bedroom in the back of the house near the kitchen. I remember my mom had it painted a neon green color and the floor was black. I had a Holly Hobby doll bedspread set. I loved that room! It was my own and I didn't have to share with my sisters. My two younger sisters shared a room, the bunk bed went into their room and they had Raggedy Ann bedspreads. Their room was painted red. Our kitchen was painted a light blue. Our front room was painted orange and we had brown furniture. My mom was and still is eclectic like that! We had a stereo and television that we entertained ourselves with but that was not all. My mom was a big reader. She always read to us and gave us tons of books. She taught us how to go to the library to check out books. We were riding the bus downtown by ourselves when I was about 10 or 11 to go to the big public library. We had at least two sets of encyclopedias that she purchased, the World Book Encyclopedias and the Funk and Wagnall's Encyclopedia set. She created our own personal library right in the foyer of our house by stacking books from the floor to the ceiling. Somewhere there is a picture on FB with me and my sisters standing in front of those books!

By the time I started going through puberty, things were rocky between my mom and "Daddy" and I know there was drug use as well. At some point, it must have gotten really bad. I remember he and one of my mother's cousins used to spend a lot of time in the bathroom. Later on I realized that they were shooting heroin. He had needle tracks on his arms. There was always a funny smell in our house when some of my older cousins and my mom's friends would come over. I realized later that it was the marijuana that they were smoking. It was no big deal to me. During that era, I guess everybody did it. But soon my mother and "Daddy" were having really bad arguments. But they were still together and I loved him. To me, everything was how it was supposed to be. One day I remember playing in the front room with my sisters and they were sitting on the couch talking and watching us play. I would organize plays and dance recitals right in the living room. My mom said to him, "Sandra needs a bra." He told me to turn around and when I did, they both looked at me and each other and she said, "I told you." Then they talked some more but I went back to playing. I thought nothing of the request. Soon after that day, early one morning, I was in bed asleep. I believe it was the weekend and he came into my room and woke me up. He said to me, "Mommy said you were growing hair down there. I want to see it." He then pulled my pajamas down and stroked me and pulled my pants back up. Then he said, "You are getting big girl." He smiled at me, pulled the covers back up and left the room. I don't know where my mother was that morning. I felt strange but also glad that he was pleased with me for growing up.

That was really the first validation I felt. I had no idea at that time that my value was not based upon my sexuality. Because we had a close relationship, I thought nothing of him looking at my body. This was my "Daddy" and he loved me. Plus, I assumed that if my mother was telling him what was happening to me, it was ok. So things went back to my normal. I continued to develop. I was still struggling in school. I was running around the neighborhood wild. I was always on punishment it seemed, meaning I couldn't come outside to play because I had gotten in trouble about doing something I wasn't supposed to. I spent a lot of this time reading the books in our home library. Reading took me to another world. I would get engrossed in books. During that time, I read the entire book of "Roots" by Alex Haley and "The Amityville Horror". I had nightmares after reading that last book but after the nightmares, I wasn't scared of horror films. I'm still not afraid but I don't watch them.

There was a book my mother had depicting drawings of sexual positions. It was called "The Joy of Sex." It was a colorful book of all kinds of positions. I was fascinated by it. I used to sneak the book into my room when no one was around. One day I got into trouble because I had mistakenly brought it to school. My teacher, a lady I hated because she was so mean, had told the class to put our books on our desks so that we could pack our bags to go home. She saw the big book on my desk and when she came to my desk and picked it up she looked at it and began yelling at me. She told me that she was calling my mother and I was going to be in big trouble. My mom came to get me and I was punished of course but it didn't faze me. I think by the time this happened, my "Daddy" was already gone. His drug habit had gotten so bad that one Christmas before his exit, all of our toys were stolen and my mother had put all of his belongings in garbage bags outside. He tried to get in the house through the back door but the chain was on it. I remember she threw an iron frying pan at the door and there was a dent in the wall. He was gone but before he was put out, he took that first sexual invasion to another level. I think at some point, my mother was working nights and he was left to watch us while she worked. They both had jobs working different shifts at the Post Office where I believe they met. I was lying in the bottom bunk bed one night in the red room and there was music in the front room playing on the stereo. I don't remember when I began sharing the bunk with my sisters but I was too big to be sleeping on the top bunk. I was laying there with my eyes closed but I hadn't gone into a deep sleep because of the loud music playing in the front room. All of a sudden, I felt someone rubbing between my buttocks. I realized that he had come into the room and as I lay on my stomach, he had his hand in my pajama pants. I didn't move but my eyes popped opened. He didn't notice and continued. I was too shocked to say anything. Then, he removed his hands and he began to use his mouth on my buttocks and rub me further between my legs. I became frightened and I must have jumped because he suddenly stopped, pulled up my pants and said, "I'm sorry, I didn't mean to scare you."

He told me to go back to sleep and kissed me on my head. Then he pulled the covers up and left the room. I don't remember if my sisters were in the top bunk or if anyone else was even in the house. But that night a shift happened in my mind about sex. My mother had conversations with us before I started puberty about sex, but they were all technical. She would show us pictures in our encyclopedias about the reproductive system and give us the proper terms but then she told us not to do it. I figured that there must have been something bad about it so I had no plans to engage in it. After that night though, I started to believed that sex was pleasurable. Although he didn't penetrate me, the feelings he invoked physically made me think that sex was good. I thought that he really loved me and touching me like that was his way of letting me know how much he loved the young woman I was becoming. I did not see how wrong it was. I am thankful that he never got the chance to go further than that. Sometimes the molester is aggressive in their attacks but often times, they are very seductive and this allows the victim to remain in their grasp because the abuse is not viewed as painful and hurtful. After my mother put him out for the drug abuse, I began to resent her because I felt that she made him leave me. I began rebelling even more. He was the only father I had ever known. For reasons I couldn't understand, he was out of my life. The relationship I had with him was what I would compare all other male relationships with later on in my life and I began to equate those similarities with love. My mother continued to work and provide for us. She did the best she could and I didn't know that she was having a major struggle herself that would culminate in her enlisting into the Army. But the incident with him was just the beginning of my foray into sex.

We always had family and friends coming over to visit. I spent days running, jumping, playing with friends from my neighborhood, staying outside playing hide and go seek until the street lights began to buzz. That was the signal to get in the house before we got in trouble. There were summer barbeques in the back yard and cousins from both sides coming over all of the time. We spent time digging in the dirt, making mud pies on the front porch in the grass and playing games.

These memories are a part of my childhood when I felt the most at peace, felt the most love from my family and the most secure. But as I grew older and developed, that dark, cloudy space in my life loomed over my head all the time. I didn't know it at the time, but the predator in our family was beginning to direct his intentions towards me. Because I was the oldest grandchild and probably spoiled, (I never considered myself as such but because of things that occurred later on, that may have been the case) I was always in the presence of the adults. I was precocious. While they were talking, playing cards, drinking, listening to music, I was in the middle making them laugh, asking questions, singing and dancing along to the music. Depending on which side of the family was there, I had some cousins that would visit who were about my age but this was my territory! For both sides of the family, 220 Custer Avenue was where the party was at. My grandfather had long moved out but for a few years he would stop by because his sister still lived on the third floor and his father would come by often. My grandmother's oldest sister lived in Linden, NJ in the suburbs. She and her husband owned a house there and he had a masonry business. This uncle and his son even redid the front porch at my grandmother's house.

I remember when they pulled up the wood steps and poured concrete and laid brick all around the front area. The steps are now slate and I remember the day that they each carved their initials into the cement when they finished. This uncle, (my great uncle) was always around fixing something or just visiting. He began renovating my grandmother's bathroom with tile at some point. I remember I would come in the bathroom just to watch him and ask him all kinds of questions. He was patient and answered them but looking back, it was like a lion sizing up his prey in a quiet, unnerving manner. He would give all of the children quarters when he came around. We would always ask for money to go buy those big brown bags of candy or get ice cream from the truck that rode up our street. His pockets were always full of change and he passed it out like water. We loved it.

He and my aunt's home in the suburbs was a simple, two story, two family home. It had a two car garage and the top floor was a rental residence. The basement was finished and it was where the children were allowed to play when visiting. He had built by hand a brick barbeque pit on the back patio where there was a finished lawn that he placed a boulder on the grass that we would always play on. When he re-bricked my grandmother's porch, he put a rock on her lawn too. There are some pictures of various cousins sitting on that rock on Facebook too! It's ironic though, how that stone on both lawns became a stone around the neck of at least two generations of women. The floor where they lived was 3 bedrooms with a living/dining room that had white furniture covered in plastic and carpeted floors. We normally spent Thanksgivings there. The children were not allowed in the living room at all. We had to eat downstairs in the basement or if it was one or two children visiting, we had to eat in the kitchen. At some point, when I was around 11 or 12 I think, I could go over to their home to help my aunt clean up her house and make a little money. She would send my uncle to pick me up from Newark on Friday evenings or Saturday mornings and help her clean. Then he would take me back home before Sunday night.

At first I had fun. She had china and silver that needed polishing. So I vacuumed, dusted, folded laundry and enjoyed cleaning up because she had good things and let me eat what I wanted. I didn't clean up well like this at home because we didn't get an allowance. In fact, we were always in trouble for not cleaning the house. For the first few visits, things were fine. I was really glad to be away from home and the money she would give me was a real plus. But soon the visits started to change. This uncle began giving me cash instead of the quarters. He would take me home and a few times, I remember that we would stop at this store on the way back to Newark. I sat in the car and he would come out and hand me five and ten dollar bills. This was when I believe he started molesting me. Those rides back home became depressing. I had totally withdrawn into myself. Sometime during those visits to clean his home is when I believe he started molesting me. I began to hate going over there. Not because I liked staying home but because I was so uncomfortable being around him.

My aunt had two mahogany and ivory statues of a man and a woman. She had a set of twins, a boy and a girl who were much older than me and she always told me that those statues represented her children. She also had a statue of Michelangelo's sculpture, The Pieta, on one of the coffee tables. She always told me to be careful when I dusted there. At first I loved looking at those sculptures and statues but I remember cleaning those statues one day when I was all by myself in the living room. All of a sudden it seemed as if the statues were coming to life. They seemed to be moving toward me. The twin statues were gyrating and coming off of the cabinet. The Pieta statue had Jesus lying on Mary's lap and there seemed to be snakes coming out from the bottom of His feet. I didn't finish cleaning that day. I began doing a poor job of cleaning everything and she was getting so upset with me. I don't think I said much to her but I was not happy anymore spending those weekends over there.

One night while I was asleep on the couch in the guest room, I woke up to the television being on. It was dark but across from the couch, sitting in the chair facing me was the twin son. He was a lot older than me and I don't remember ever feeling uncomfortable around him. He was sitting on the chair and he had to have been watching me sleep. I remember feeling angry that he was there watching tv while I was asleep and I began huffing and wrestling with the covers. He finally got up and left the room. I don't know what he was doing in there or what his intentions were, but I was really angry with him afterwards. Thinking back, I remember prior to that night, all of us were over there for a family a BBQ and it was dark outside but we had the flood lights on out back and music was playing. I was dancing to the song, "Get Off" and I remember I was having a good time but when I looked his way, he was staring at me. I don't know what he was thinking about while he was watching, but that night on the couch, I believe God didn't allow anything to happen to me by his hand. Eventually I stopped going over there. But that uncle was still coming over and being around the kids. He had a yellow Ford pickup truck that he used for his business. He would take different groups of nieces and nephews mulberry picking in little towns some Saturday mornings. We would sit in the back of the truck and depending on which side of the family was visiting that day, there was no question of who got to sit on the wheel hump. This was before the days of child restraint laws. It was always me and one of the cousins my age that ruled the roost in the back of that pickup truck. We bounced and sang crazy kid songs until we arrived at the orchards and came back home full of mulberries, clothes stained from eating handfuls of fruit, and grass and dirt stains from running all over the orchard. It was fun, until one day, the fun stopped for me.

We had gone picking and I really don't remember which group of children went that day. I must have been about 11 or 12. I know two of my sisters were there and when we got to the orchard, we all jumped out running to start picking. How he and I ended up between the trees alone is a mystery, but I remember none of the other kids were near by. I do remember staring up into the sky because somehow I was looking up at him from a kneeling position on the ground. The memory is that the sky was cloudy even though I know it had to be a bright sunny day and I could see him, but his face is blacked out. I believe that this incident pushed me completely into the dark hole that sometimes happens when a child is molested. They disappear inside themselves to hide from the pain. Then they act out in various ways as an outcry but often times, it goes unnoticed. What child knows how to tell someone else that an adult who was supposed to love and protect them has violated them? That someone has forced them to perform perverted physical acts that made their skin crawl or caused them to feel dirty and ashamed?

For me, I felt shameful and worthless even the more. I began to believe that the only way I could feel loved was to engage in sexual activity. I don't remember how long we were out in the orchard, but I remember riding back home sitting with my head on my hand as my arm was leaning on the side of the truck. I had totally withdrawn into myself. That darkness was surrounding me. I heard my sisters and the other children laughing and playing but there was no joy to be found for me.

From that moment on, I was only concerned with finding love through sexual activity anyway I thought I could get it. I lived on a street where there were a lot of kids. I played with most of them. Some were my age, some were older and some were younger. There was a mixture of boys and girls. We had lots of fun playing various games. Before this last incident took place, we would all pretend to be television characters like Wonder Woman, Isis, Batman and Robin, Superman. We played Hide and Seek, Freeze Tag, and 1, 2, 3 Red Light. It was fun and we mostly got along really well. But then, somewhere along the line, those games became sexual. I had begun running rampant of course, with puberty in full force now.

Soon after that incident, I thought that I was pretty grown because now I had to wear a bra and I had long legs and a little bump in the back. I was really a tomboy, but I thought that I was cute and because I could run with the best of the boys, you couldn't tell me anything! By then, the boys had begun to explore by running up and swatting girls on the butt. I knew all about the changes my body was going through because of the talks my mom had with me and my sisters. But I had no idea what to do with all of the emotions that were attached to those changes. So what did I do? If I liked a boy, I would allow him to touch me. I was bold and if he told me he liked me, he could go just a little further.

There were many incidents of me being caught in the back yard or between the garage and the fence. Because my mother and grandmother were always working, I would sneak a boy into the doorway of our house on the first floor if I could get away with it, or in the stairwell of the hall leading to the second floor where my grandmother lived. Sometimes one of my sisters would catch me. I could threaten the one right behind me, but my next to the youngest would broadcast it with an "ooooo, I'm telling mommy!" So I was always in trouble.

Sometime in the fall of 1979, just before I turned 13 years old, a new family moved onto my block and there was a boy in the family who I thought was the cutest thing ever. He was so cool that all the other boys looked up to him and all the girls smiled when he came up the street to play. He ran the fastest, could dance the best and became the ring leader of the boys. I had the biggest crush on him and although I was a tomboy, I flirted with him all the time. My reputation by then, was being known as the "fast" girl on the block. I'm sure the other boys told him about me, so I don't know what he thought of me. But pretty soon, he and I were boyfriend and girlfriend. I was in love! I was ecstatic when we started going together. Of course, soon afterwards, he began trying to persuade me to have sex with him. Although I was promiscuous, I was technically still a virgin. No one had gotten that far.

Soon, I concocted this bright idea that for my 13th birthday, I would have sex with him 13 times. Now where I got this notion from, I can't tell you. I was in love and he was asking about the two of us going beyond the bumping and grinding that I had been doing with other boys. Remember, I was doing anything I could to find the love that I equated sex with. So a few weeks before my 13th birthday, I decided that it was time to lose my virginity. My grandmother's house had a partially finished basement. It was our favorite place to play for a while. My mother and her siblings played down there. It had concrete floors with the poles that held up the house down the middle of it. It had been painted bright yellow at one time and my mom and her cousins made it psychedelic by painting peace signs and hand prints all over it. We used to roller skate down there too. Then, it became a storage place because people put furniture, boxes and other things they stopped using there.

It was down in that dusty old basement that I had my first sexual intercourse experience. It was a tender moment, although I didn't realize that it would be painful. He was gentle with me and I thought this was what true love felt like. I even told him that I wish we could be together for the rest of our lives. What in the world did I know at 13? Thus continued the foray into seeking love through sex, not understanding or learning until years later that real love is more than what you feel when you physically engage with a person. True love is about so much more and it goes way beyond sex. I didn't have a clue. I had never seen it in action and I had no pattern to follow.

My family had been destroyed by this perverted cycle and no one understood the Biblical example found in 2 Corinthians 13:4-5, "Love is patient, kind, not envious, not puffed up, doesn't behave unseemly, seeks not her own, is not easily provoked, thinks no evil, does not rejoice in sin but rejoices in truth, bears all things, believes all things, hopes in all things and endures all things." Don't get me wrong, we loved one another as family, but that love was also fragile. You see, my mother was known as the "black sheep" of the family. She had my sisters and I at a young age and we all had different fathers. My grandmother had my mother as a teenager but she and my grandfather married young and although he had children by other women, he was only married to my grandmother. So my mother coming up pregnant at a young age must not have been received well. Of course, the abuse she suffered by the uncle was likely the main factor, but the problem was swept under the rug. This man had abused his own daughter and nothing was done about it to my knowledge. All I know is that this aunt and uncle and their children lived in a nicer town away from the rest of the family with their own business and they drove Cadillacs, had plastic covered couches and if you went there to visit, you couldn't go in the living room if you were a child. There were no such rules at my grandmother's house. Kids were everywhere. The adults sometimes were loud, cussing and fussing but we did have a sense of security. Even though there was arguing, we stuck together. I remember one night, I think in the summer, one of my aunts was down the street and had gotten into a fight with a girl who came from a big family. We were on the porch when someone got there to tell us and my grandmother went inside the house, got a steel bat and went running down the street. The kids were told to stay on the porch and she came back a little while later with the bat and a scar on her knee. Let me tell you, that woman is a little spitfire! Her hair is white now but even now, you don't mess with her or her family!

And so, the countdown began with me and my boyfriend to get to the number 13. We got all the way to the number 7 I believe. I had gotten my period around that time and because of those encyclopedias, I knew all about it. It was no big deal to me because I had read about it. My mom had explained what would happen and that was that. I didn't really equate sex with pregnancy so when I missed my period, I wasn't a big deal to me. Then I started getting sick, (which I didn't know was morning sickness). I guess my mom started watching me closely and she looked at me one day and the next thing I know, we are at the doctor's office. I had to stay home from school and of course that didn't bother me one bit. I remember coming home early and going upstairs to my grandmother's and she asked why I was home. I unabashedly told her that I had to go to the doctor because I had a knot in my stomach. I believe one of my aunts was in the front room with us. I remember that as soon as I said it, it got quiet as a mouse in there.

A few days afterward, my mother had the come to Jesus meeting with me. I realized I was pregnant and although I knew all of the technical things, I had no clue what it really meant. She first asked me whose baby was it. I lied and said it was an older boy who lived around the corner because I knew that she would make me stop seeing my boyfriend. Then she said to me the words that I will never forget. She asked me if I wanted to keep the baby, but if I kept the baby, I would have hell to pay. I really thought that I would get kicked out of the house. Although I didn't know what it entailed, I told her I didn't want to keep it. She said ok and went back to her reading. I walked around in total ignorance until the day of the appointment arrived. We went to the doctor's office and I remember her sitting in the room with me while the doctor examined and prepped me. He had to place suppositories in me to induce labor. I wouldn't cooperate and I remember a nurse was holding me down and saying, "That's why you need to keep your legs closed!" I was suffering miserably.

When the pain got bad, my mother ended up stepping out of the room. All I remember is the sad, stern look she had on her face. I endured that experience all alone. It felt as though I was being ripped apart in the middle. It was the worst experience I ever had. When it was all over, my mom came back in the room but I had already shut the world out. Things between us weren't the same anymore. I loved my mother and always will, but after that incident, we drifted even farther apart. I'm sure she was disappointed in me, but I felt all alone and ashamed and the hurt was deep. She had already made my "daddy" leave, and now she made me go through this painful experience.

I went home and everything was mentally dark for me. But after a few weeks, I was ready to start having sex again. I hadn't yet told my boyfriend, but I did tell a few friends. I was on punishment and couldn't come out, but I remember the day he found out. He was so mad that he sped off down the street on his bike. I felt horrible and we didn't talk for months. When we finally did, he forgave me and we started having sex again. He began using condoms, but we weren't feeling the same anymore. I think we had sex about twice more and then our relationship was over. He had even began chasing another girl who started coming to our neighborhood. I began to get jealous and would spend hours inside the house crying whenever I saw him playing with her. I stopped coming outside as often. This heartbreak propelled me further into seeking love and validation through sex.

By the time, I was about to enter 8th grade, my mother had decided to join the Army and leave us with my grandfather. Remember he hadn't been around the house much after he moved out. We would visit him where he lived with whatever girlfriend he had at the time. It seemed like one day out of the blue, she took us to see him and this lady who was his latest girlfriend and she told us that we were going to live with him because she was joining the Army. I had no clue what any of it meant but I just took it as, "She is leaving me with this strange man and his girlfriend." I was really numb to every thing that was going around me. She began preparing us to move in with him.

We ended up living on the third floor of a house similar to my grandmother's across town from her. I didn't question why we weren't staying with my grandmother or someone else in our family. The decision was made and I didn't question anything. Once we got settled into the apartment, I remember my mom taking us downtown on the bus with a backpack on. She had given us each $5.00 and she kept talking about how she wanted us to be good in school and behave ourselves and that she was going to come back for us. She had taken us to the new school that we would be attending before she left and showed us the bus route. She was preparing us for her departure, but I was in my own world. I was dealing with too much of my own pain to notice hers.

Looking back years later, I thought about the day she took us to the Federal Building downtown with that backpack on and kissed us goodbye, telling us to be good as she instructed us to take the down elevator because she was going upstairs to be sworn in. I remember standing in front of the elevator door watching it as it closed and seeing the look on her face as it closed on her four little girls. I didn't think about it then, but when I became a woman and a mother to my own children, I realized that she may have looked fine on the outside, but her heart had to be breaking as she got on that elevator leaving her four girls behind. I now realize that was probably the hardest and the scariest thing she has ever had to do. At age 14, I had no idea what kind of sacrifice that took for her to leave us behind. After the door closed on us, my sisters and I took the elevator down, got on the bus after stopping at the fresh fruit stand to each buy a brown bag of cherries and go back to our new home with our grandfather and "granny". I don't remember shedding a tear. We had money in our pocket and were taking the bus back home. My sisters and I ate all of those cherries and we got home and had the biggest stomach aches ever! We had stuff coming from both ends and for the moment, I wasn't thinking about my mom.

We then began settling down with our new home, neighborhood and school. Our apartment was four rooms - a kitchen, small living area and two small bedrooms that were connected by a doorway. My sisters and I slept in the smaller room on twin beds with only room for a small dresser. My grandfather and his girlfriend's room was right next to ours with their bed and a dresser. We had a couch and a coffee table in the living area and a small table in the kitchen. There was one bathroom that was in the back of the kitchen and the back door was right outside of it. The walls were slanted in all of the rooms except the kitchen.

The owner of the house was a friend of my grandfather and the people on the second floor had 3 boys that were close to my sister's ages. There were other kids on the block that we got to know. There was a large field next to our house where the kids on the block played baseball. We took the bus to the Catholic School that my mom enrolled us in before she left. We were seemingly adjusting to everything, but my grandfather and his girlfriend drank a lot. We would have moments where everything would be fine. We had a radio in the living area and we would dance and listening to music, making up dance routines and singing like we used to when we lived on Custer Avenue. I was in the eighth grade and we wore uniforms. We had to get up early in the morning before first light. My grandfather got up early and we had to be up and dressed before he left for work. It was too early for us and for a time, he would get us up and head out to work. Somewhere down the line, he had begun yelling and and cussing at us when we didn't get up right away. We had begun getting to school late because we would fall asleep after he left. His girlfriend worked at a Head Start center and I don't remember him ever taking us to school. When he started getting phone calls about our tardiness, he would get mad at us and yell some more. I started running wild around the neighborhood but was not sexually active with any of the boys.

I really missed my old friends. A few of the kids from our old neighborhood attended our Catholic School so we didn't feel too uncomfortable. In fact, before we moved, I had attended a school dance there and met a boy that later became my boyfriend. He was nice. We spent a lot of time on the phone and talking on the playground. The only time we were somewhere alone, was one day when I was upset because I thought one of the boys from the old neighborhood had told him about the abortion I had. I was crying and mad at him but he didn't know anything about what happened. I was probably overreacting and he and I met in the stairwell afterschool to talk. I remember us kissing and he whispered in my ear that I was his "beautiful orange blossom". That was the sweetest thing any boy had ever told me. I felt loved. We continued to talk for a few months but we didn't stay boyfriend and girlfriend for long.

At home things were getting rough. With both of them drinking, there were nights of arguing. Sometimes it would spill over onto us. Granny began telling us that nobody in our family wanted us. Grandad began complaining about how our mother wasn't sending him any money to take care of us. Sometimes they would be up all night arguing and we still had to get up to go to school. My grandfather was what they used to call a "rolling stone". The reason my grandparents were no longer together were because of his infidelity. He always had different girlfriends that he lived with before we lived with him. I remember once Granny had gotten sick and and had to go into the hospital. One night while she was in the hospital, he didn't come home until the wee hours of the morning. I remember her calling and I spoke to her and told her that he wasn't home. I was sitting right on the bed next to the phone and he wasn't there. Later on that evening, he had come home and we were supposed to have done our chores, which we didn't and he yelled at us. Granny called him and they were arguing. It was late and he came in the room yelling at me saying, "Why did you tell that woman that I wasn't home!". I tried explaining that he wasn't when I talked to her and he took the guitar that our mom had brought us before she left and hit me across the legs with it. It broke on the handle. I remember having a bruise on my leg from that. I was crying, but I was mad because he was saying I was lying about him not being home. I know he was not home when I spoke to her.

I loved my grandfather, but it took a while for me to get to know him. He was in the background of my life and then all of a sudden, he was right there in my face. It took a minute for me to get comfortable with him. He was mostly quiet but once we got used to each other, I realized that he loved us. In our yard, he had planted a garden and there were grape harbors, pear and peach trees. I would spend time with him in the garden and he would teach me about the strawberries, peppers, squash and okras he had planted there. We didn't talk a lot about things that most children would talk to their grandparents about. I think that we just were trying to make the most out of the situation that we found ourselves in.

Granny and I talked sometimes. She tried to be a friend to me and teach me girl things. The lady downstairs from us had a son who came to visit during the summer that I had a crush on. One summer night we ended up sitting under the pear tree in the back yard kissing and we got busted. Later Granny and I laughed about it because we were sitting where the dog would poop. She yelled at me when it happened, but afterwards we had a pretty good laugh. Once when we were in the kitchen preparing dinner, we begun laughing and playing. She was making pork chops and I ended up with flour all over my hands. I was playing with my sisters and had flour handprints all over them. I decided to go into grandad's room and hold his cheeks putting flour all over his face. He turned around and began whooping my behind, yelling until granny told him I was finished cooking. He was pissed off because we were playing with food that we were supposed to be cooking. We often got whipped when we didn't clean up, which was most of the time. We hated cleaning up and when we lived with my mom, we always got in trouble for not cleaning up. We would stay up late at night washing dishes because nobody cleaned up after dinner.

Towards the end of my eighth-grade year, our school sponsored a Cotillion. I wanted to go because everyone in my class would be there and some of my friends were a part of the Cotillion court. I couldn't do that part because we didn't have the money for me to participate. But I begged and pleaded to attend, so Granny made my grandad buy me a dress and get my hair done. I was so glad to be going to the Cotillion and felt so special. My grandmother and aunts and uncles had begun visiting after the initial tension about my mom leaving us with my grandfather dissipated. So I went to get my hair done by the cousin who used to shut herself in the bathroom on Custer with my "dad". She worked in a salon and did my hair. My grandfather had taken us all shopping for a dress at the mall. They bought me a teal colored gown that had a pleated bottom and puffy sleeves. I had a colorful wrap to go with it. I got all dressed up to go to this Cotillion. I felt like Cinderella when I went inside because my friends didn't recognize me at first. I got there late and it was dark in the room because the program had already started. When my friends did recognize me, they were awed that I looked so beautiful. I had on a little makeup and they were gushing all over me. Imagine my surprise when my first love walked up to me. I had no idea that he would be there. He was looking at me and had the biggest smile on his face and I knew that I was beautiful at that moment.

It turns out that he rode with some of the kids from my old neighborhood. When it was time to go, he talked me into riding with them to my old block. I called my grandad and told him I was going to my grandmother's house after the Cotillion and my friends were going to drop me off over there. I got in the car and ended up sitting on his lap because there was not a lot of room in the car. He began whispering to me about how beautiful I was and talked me into coming back to his house. It wasn't too late but it was getting dark. He told me his mother was at work and wouldn't be home so I went to his house. Of course, we started kissing and he began feeling me up, but he noticed I was shaking. He asked me if I was I ok. I missed him but was really nervous because I was afraid of getting pregnant again.

I hadn't had sex since the abortion. He stopped and we began to talk. He told me that he didn't want me to be afraid of him. We decided not to go any further and he walked me to my grandmother's house. I told her that I had just come from the school's Cotillion and wanted to spend the night at her house. I went home the next day and no one was the wiser. I was still wary of getting pregnant again, but there was an older boy across the street from my grandad's house who was cute and began to talk to me all the time. He would see me sitting on the porch and stop and talk to me. Just having light conversation but he did ask me if I had a boyfriend. I told him no, but when he realized I was much younger than him, he told me that he would be my boyfriend when I was at least a sophomore. He was almost out of high school. Whenever I walked past his house, if he was outside on the porch with his friends, he would say, "Hey Sandra!" and I would blush.

Even though I thought a few of the boys in this neighborhood were cute, I didn't have sex with any of them. I did go with a girl who lived around the corner to one of their houses and me and the boy ended up grinding in his room but that was as far as it went. I remember I had a pair of panties that had some lace on them that granny had bought me. He thought they were sexy. It wasn't until I started in high school that I had sex again. One of the girls that lived across the street from me was a Christian. We all played together but she wore skirts all the time, didn't cuss and was always telling us about the Bible.

She and I became close and I had begun spending time in her house asking questions about God. Her brother was cute and I had a crush on him, and he was a Christian too. He was always reading the Bible. She even began taking me to her church. I remember on the first visit I had at her church, I was listening to the singing and the preaching and my leg started shaking while I was in my seat. I couldn't control it. I had this strange feeling come over me but I didn't know what was going on.

I didn't go with her often but whenever I did, I enjoyed it. Soon after, she invited me to a revival. We took the bus with her brother to the tent that was set up outside at the park downtown and I had that feeling again while listening to the preacher. I started crying and when the preacher asked who wanted to be saved, I went along with everyone else down front. My friend went with me and she was shouting and raising her hands in the air. I put my hands up and repeated what the preacher told us to. When we finished, he told us that we were saved. My friend grabbed me and hugged me and we started crying again. I was saved and it felt awesome! It was the most peace I had felt in a long time. The next morning as I was looking out my back window at the field next to our house, I saw my friend's brother walking and yelled "hello". He looked up and waved back and he shouted, "Are you still running for the Lord?" I said yes and he went on his way. I believed I was saved but had no idea what that meant. My friend tried to get me to join her church and was very encouraging to me but I was still having struggles. She didn't know what I had been through because I had never told her. I didn't go back with her to church and eventually, I was back doing the same things as before.

At the end of my eighth-grade year, there was a graduation ceremony. This class was the last class to graduate from this school because the church was closing the school. We were having our ceremony in the cathedral, which is huge. It is a landmark in the city of Newark. In fact, one of the Popes came for a historic visit before we attended the school. The church takes up a whole city block and the stained glass windows were made in replica to windows in the Roman Basilica. There were tall towers and the inside had marble stairs leading to the pulpit area and beautiful carvings all over the building. I was excited about this graduation and I thought my mom would be able to come home for it. I think she was trying, but it wasn't until the morning of my graduation that I realized that she wouldn't be there. I had to be at the church early and my grandmother was going to take me there so I had to walk to her house. I remember waiting outside on her porch crying as I waited for her to come downstairs to take me to school because I was sad that my mom wasn't going to make it. However, I got through the ceremony as sad as I was. I know my grandmother and one of my aunts were, there but I don't recall seeing them in the audience. It was all a blur until it was over. I remember walking out of the church with my classmates and as we were coming down the steps, I noticed my grandad and granny standing outside of the station wagon we had with my sisters holding a vase full of red roses. They hadn't made it to the ceremony, but they stopped and got me flowers. I was happy that they made it. We ended up going to our house and it seemed as if a truce was called and everyone got along well. I was still sad that my mom couldn't be there, but I enjoyed the small celebration we had.

It wasn't until almost the end of summer I think, that my mom was able to get home. She had finished basic training and was able to come home in time to enroll me in the magnet school that I was accepted into for the fall. She took me to enroll in Science High School. I wasn't sure if

I really wanted to go there at first. I applied to the Arts High School but was scared to audition. I would have to stand in front of people and sing and although I loved singing, I wasn't confident enough to do it in front of an audience. Who knows where I would be now if I had the guts to go to that audition? In any case, my mom got me registered into the Science School. We walked around campus and my mom was speaking to a lot of the kids because she knew some of them from the neighborhood. I felt a little uneasy being with her. She looked better and she seemed happy, but I was feeling abandoned and let down after she didn't come to my graduation. I didn't feel comfortable around her anymore. While we were at the school, a boy came up and spoke to her. I didn't pay him much attention until she introduced us and he told her that he would help me when school started. I don't remember how she knew him but it seemed as if he began following us around.

He was a junior and I was a freshman. He introduced me to a few people at the school. I knew one boy from my old neighborhood who attended the school and I had a cousin who was also a student there, but I didn't know anyone else. By the time I started my freshman year, the boy my mom introduced me to during registration had become my boyfriend. As soon as school started, he began riding the bus with me home. One day we ended up in the basement of my house having sex. Sometimes I would ride the bus to his house and we would do it there. He lived in a very big house and his mom was a teacher. She seemed ok with the idea of me being her son's girlfriend. My mom had to return to her next duty station and soon afterwards, we moved into a bigger apartment in a nicer neighborhood. We lived on the second floor of a three family house. We still had to take the bus to school but because my high school was downtown, I had to travel further away than my sisters. They attended school in the neighborhood even though my next to the youngest ended up going to the school closer towards my grandmother's home. There was some sort of attendance zone mix up and she had to walk to and from school by herself for a little bit. My boyfriend and I were really involved by this time. I spent a lot of time at his house and since it was around the corner from my grandmother's house, I was over there often. We got along well but I was insecure. At school we were sweethearts, but I would get jealous because of some of the girls he knew at school. There was even one girl on his block who I was jealous of and we argued about it. She was nice but I always thought something was going on between the two of them. One day we all sat down and she told me that the two of them were like brother and sister and she really liked me and wanted to be my friend. After that, she and I got along and he and I stopped arguing about it.

The following school year, I was a sophomore and he was a senior about to graduate. We were doing well and we were using condoms most of the times when we had sex but we slipped up and I became pregnant. I panicked and didn't know what to do. I told him and we decided not to keep the baby. I didn't want to keep it but I was really terrified of having another abortion. I don't think I told him about the first one, but that was what we agreed to do. I was going to get the procedure done and we were going to go on as if nothing happened. I backed out at the last minute and told my grandad and granny that I was pregnant. I remember they were in bed and she was sitting on the side smoking a cigarette. I thought my grandad was asleep. I began to tell her and she started shaking him up telling him to get up. She asked him, "Didn't you hear this girl say she is pregnant?". He was grumbling, "Well what the f*** you want me to do?" She sent me to my room and they began arguing. After a few hours had gone by, she called me back to her room and he was laying down watching tv. She said, "You're going to have this baby and go back to school. You ain't the first to get pregnant. We're going to take care of this baby and you're going to finish school." She told me to call my boyfriend and tell him and his mother to come over.

The next day, I called him and told him that they knew. He was upset because we had agreed to abort the baby. But finally he said he would tell his mom. I don't know how she reacted, but a few days later, everyone came to our house. I know there was a lot of talking among the adults, but I don't remember much of anything else. I did sleep and eat a lot. I had to stop going to regular school and ended up enrolling in an unwed mothers school. I hated going to that school. At home I was frustrated. All I did was eat, sleep and lay around. My sisters were probably as miserable as I was because I didn't do much around the house using the old pregnancy excuse so they had to pick up my slack. I got yelled at for eating stuff my grandfather brought home that he wanted for himself. Granny would take up for me and I know that made it worse. But I went along like this until the evening of April 27, 1983.

I kept feeling like I had to use the bathroom but every time tried, nothing would happen. I wasn't in any pain, I just felt this pressure on my bladder. At some point, I went back to the bathroom and all of a sudden water gushed out and I began having this extreme pain. I yelled and granny came in the bathroom yelling, "Dickie, get up, this girl is getting ready to have this baby!" Immediately chaos ensued. I was heading to the hospital. One of my sisters went upstairs to the neighbors who we had become close with to tell them what was happening. The lady came to sit with my sisters. We got to the hospital and I was rolled into delivery. I was placed in stirrups and the process began. I was in the room by myself with the doctor and nurses urging me to push. I was too busy screaming. The nurse had to tell me how to breath and push. She kept slapping me on my thigh when I wouldn't cooperate. She kept trying to get me to look up in the mirror to watch the baby come out, but I was too afraid. Finally, sometime before midnight, I pushed one last time and the doctor told me that I had a baby boy. I heard him cry and saw him as they laid him on my stomach. He didn't look like a baby to me at first, but when they cleaned him up and brought him wrapped in a blanket, I was in awe. I wanted my boyfriend to see him. I got misty eyed when I was looking at him. My grandfather came into the recovery room after a while and when I saw him, he had the biggest grin on his face. I asked had anyone called my boyfriend and he told me that they were going to call him in the morning. I saw my son once more before they wheeled me into recovery.

Later the next day, my boyfriend and his mother came to the hospital. The nurses had rolled the bassinet into my room. My boyfriend's mother and my grandparents were talking in the hall at one point and the two of us were in the room with this newborn baby. I remember looking at my boyfriend holding our son up and nuzzling his cheeks. I thought it was a perfect picture but I had no clue as to what I was supposed to do with this baby. So off we go into the sunset, baby in arms, ready to be parents and take on the world. Too bad we bumbled along the way.

When I got home and had to spend those first few days with the baby alone, I was a wreck. He cried, I was overwhelmed with feeding, diapering, keeping him clean and trying to return to normal. I remember my granny fussing when I didn't clean up the bottles and change him in a timely manner. I didn't know how to handle all of the pressure. I didn't go back to school right away because the school year was almost ending. Not long after that, my mother came home on leave and we prepared to move into a house farther away from my grandmother. It was a big 3 bed room 2 story house with a garage, basement and attic. It was a beautiful house. I enrolled in the local high school with one of my sisters. I was a sophomore and was behind but I went to school in the fall. The boyfriend that I had in eighth grade attended the same high school and we remained friends. My baby's father was getting ready to graduate and was making plans to go to college. A few months after our son was born, we started having sex and I soon got pregnant again. I could not keep this child and talked to his mother and she helped me arrange to have an abortion. I went through with it this time and immediately went into a deep depression. I barely took care of my son. Most of the times, my boyfriend's mom would take him to her house. I wouldn't do anything at home and it caused a lot of arguments between my grandad and granny.

This whole time frame was a blur. I couldn't tell if I was coming or going. Finally, the end of the school year was approaching. I was doing horribly in school myself and my boyfriend was preparing to attend college in a town that was at least a few hours away from me. I was really sad. I was mad at him and we argued a lot. I felt as if he was abandoning me. We had gone to his prom together. My cousin did my hair again and my uncle's wife took me shopping and got me a navy blue dress with sequins and lace. I loved it and had a good time at the prom with him but as it got closer to graduation, we drew further apart. I had become close with his mother and often talked to her about how I was feeling. She was trying to reassure me that he wasn't abandoning me and that it would be ok. The day that he left for college, I rode with them to take him to his dorm.

I remember when we were driving back, I was sitting in the backseat and I had withdrawn into myself like I always did when things were hurting me and she said, 'What's wrong, your boo boo left you?". She was teasing and I don't think she was being mean, but I took it that way. After he left, I decided that I would start looking for another boyfriend. My son was around 6 to 7 months old. His grandmother had put him in a daycare and she kept encouraging me to finish school. I really tried to but my mind was not on finishing school. I was tired of being lonely and I began talking to a few guys that I knew. In fact, one day I went over to her house and called one of them while I was there. I thought about my boyfriend but figured he was seeing other people as well. Things at home were getting bad and I was getting yelled at a lot.

It all came to a head one night when we were at a friend of my granny's house and a shouting match ensued. The next thing I knew, my grandmother had taken me and my son with her to her house and I began living with her again. I don't remember if she was already at this lady's house or she was called, but I remember it was a huge commotion. I was kind of glad to be back living with my grandmother. I missed her terribly. She has been the most constant in my life. Even when I didn't actually live with her, she always found a way to stay in touch with me. Throughout all of the years she has always been a source of peace and comfort for me. In fact, even as I am writing this, a song is on Pandora that I learned while listening to her records. She attends the church that my great-grandparents went to. She was in the choir and she had a collection of gospel records that she often listened to and sang along with. One of the first gospel music artists that I loved listening to is Richard Smallwood. The song playing is I Love the Lord. It is strange (not really, that's GOD!) that while I am writing this portion of my story, this song comes on and I am taken back to the times that God ministered to me while listening to this song in my grandmother's living room!

And so, with a little relief, I moved back into my grandmother's house. She enrolled me in the high school the following school semester and I began as a Junior. I was always smart, but the things that I had endured caused me not to focus. My mother instilled in us early on that we were intelligent and she always provided us with activities that broadened our perspectives. She was our Girl Scout Troop leader when we were little. Remember the cookies? She brought us science kits, encyclopedias, crafting supplies, tons of books and music. We were enrolled in ballet (my sister) and violin classes. We went to the museum and the library by ourselves. My mother had a lot of emotional pain from the abuse that she suffered at the hands of that family member, but she made sure that we had access to resources that would enable us to expand our thinking. She always talked to us in an intelligent way. When we were little, she would give us cooking lessons in the kitchen and we would learn how to measure. Those things stayed with me even after she went away from us.

I began the next school year but I was still looking for love. Some of my friends on my old street that were my age had gone away to school, some were still in high school, but I was a young mother now. By now, my son spent more time in day care and with his grandmother than with me. My grandmother didn't let me go anywhere without taking him with me. She would tell me that I had the baby so it was my responsibility to take care of him. She helped buy diapers and groceries but she made sure that I cleaned up after myself and kept him clean. I did a lot better because she did not tolerate me being lazy. I lived there with my grandmother and my aunt who was next to the youngest of my grandparent's children. My aunt had left her husband who was physically abusing her. In our talks later on while living there, I heard about the molestation that other family members endured by this uncle. My aunt and I became closer for a spell, but just before I moved to Texas, our relationship crumbled and we stopped getting along. But it was only for a time. We have since reconciled.

My focus was definitely not on school. It was my mission to find love and I was so determined that I remember one day walking up the street to the store with one of my cousins, telling her during our conversation that "the next relationship I get in will be for keeps." Talk about a self-fulfilling prophecy, that is precisely what happened! Little did I know that I was about to endure physical and emotional abuse from someone that I loved the most and who "loved" me. There was a young lady who lived across the street from me growing up. She was a few years older than I and even though occasionally all of the kids on our street played together, sometimes she spent time doing things that I wasn't old enough to do. She was able to stay out later, she could wear makeup and was allowed to go further away from home than I was. She had two older brothers that I had a crush on, but I was too young at the time to get involved with either of them. By the time I moved back to my old neighborhood, I was "mature" enough to hang out with her. One day, I was at her house and she was talking on the phone with a male friend. She told me that he wanted to say hello so I got on the phone. This friend of hers said hello and he had a deep voice. That piqued my interest and we talked for a bit. Then between my friend and I, we arranged a time that we could meet. He lived across the highway and she agreed that we would walk over to his house one day so that I could meet him face to face.

One Friday afternoon, after school was out and my son was at his grandmothers, she and I walked to his house. I remember I had my hair in a shag jheri curl. I also wore glasses. I had on a pair of tight jeans and a plaid shirt with a green sweat shirt over the top and a pair of black boots. Now remember I was a tomboy but by this time, I had grown out of it mostly. I knew that I was cute and sashayed around thinking I was the stuff. When we got to his house, we went in the hallway and this guy was waiting for us. He was tall, had on a brown suit with a tan crew neck shirt underneath, some brown kicks, with a Kangol hat and shades on. He looked cute to me even though I couldn't see his eyes and I liked the sound of his voice already from talking on the phone. My friend decided to go upstairs and speak to his father and he and I went to sit in his brother's van that was parked outside. We began talking and I was mesmerized by his voice. He was telling me that he was a musician and played for a church. He was six years older than me so I thought, "Wow, a real man!" I told him about my son and he told me he had a daughter but he wasn't with her mother. We must have stayed in that van for over and hour because it was beginning to get dark.

Eventually, we got out of the van and went into the hallway. He yelled up the stairs for my friend to come down. He had his shades on the whole time and so I asked him to let me see his eyes. When he took off his shades, you could have knocked me over with a feather! He had the prettiest brown eyes I had ever encountered on a guy. I had to hold on to the handrail! When my friend came down, we exchanged numbers and hugged. He smelled so good. I was done after meeting him. On the way home, talking to my friend, I told her I was ready to become involved with him. We talked on the phone for a few days and I invited him to a football game at school. We met and began the walk to the football stadium behind the school. He told me that no girl had ever invited him to a football game. He said he liked me because I was different and asked me to be his girlfriend. I said yes and we kissed for the first time. I was on cloud 9! Here I was, a 16-year-old dating a guy who had a job and was six years older. We talked over the phone for a few weeks and I was telling all my family and friends that I was in love.

Looking back, my naivety was probably showing but nobody could tell me anything. Remember, I was the oldest grandchild and I spent a lot of years around my my aunts, uncle and older cousins. I guess they were a little indulgent of me now that I think about it. My aunts, uncle and older cousins were always taking me places and doing things with me. Not always just me, of course, but I spent a lot of time with them. So even when I became a mom, I was still close to them. My uncle's wife and I became very close and she was always someone I could talk to about everything, including boys. I actually had a big crush on her youngest brother. She had a great influence on me. At the beginning of my relationship with my "new" boyfriend, things were ok. For a few weeks we would talk on the phone or I would go to his house after school. Then one day, he called me and told me he had to go out of town with his pastor. He asked me to come over his house and I said yes.

When I got there he began telling me how much he would miss me because he had fallen in love with me. Of course that is what I was longing to hear. We began hugging and kissing and of course, we had sex for the first time. Even though I had sex before, none of my partners were experienced enough to make me feel the way he did. The feelings were very strong and I believed that I had finally found the love I had been seeking for so long. He went out of town, (I found out years later that he really didn't go out of town, he just wanted to have sex with me!) came back and he began taking me to dinner, buying me clothes and I started going with him to church. But then he started become very possessive of me. Like if I didn't come over to his house right after school, he would be upset. I was trying to spend time with my son on some days. He would get mad if I dropped my son off to his grandmother's house saying that I was going over there to be with my ex-boyfriend.

I still talked to my ex's mom and we had a good relationship even though her son and I weren't together anymore so I thought. He was still in school and seemed to be doing well. I had moved on. One day I had taken my son over to my new boyfriend's house and he told me he didn't want me to bring him over there anymore. I was confused and a little hurt but I took him back home. My grandmother didn't want me to take him over there either. She never seemed to warm up to this man and I couldn't figure out why she didn't like him. She told me that I needed to leave him alone (along with everyone else) but I kept insisting I was in love. It didn't take long for his possessiveness to turn violent. It started off with subtle threats. He was living with his father and one of his older brothers. I was a quiet person around people I didn't know. So whenever I went over to his house, we spent most of our time in his room. I would speak to his father and brother if they were in the front when I came in but that was it. He had began asking me what I was looking at whenever were out together. If we walked past another guy, he would say things like, "You must want to be with him you looking so hard." I would always say no and he would tell me to stop checking other guys out so I began walking around with my head down. It finally came to a head one day while we were in his kitchen and he was cooking something. His father was in there talking with us at first and his brother was going in and out the whole time. Finally, his father went to his room in the back of the house and we were alone. He asked me what was I looking at and began accusing me of checking out his brother. He was in my face calling me a whore, saying he was tired of me always checking other guys out. I was trying to convince him that I wasn't interested in his brother when all of a sudden, he smacked me. I had been standing by the kitchen window and he had me cornered there near the sink. I was shocked and afraid because it was if he had turned into another person. I cried out but no one came to my rescue. I was covering my face with my hands and he told me to get out of his house. I left hurting and confused because I loved him and really wanted to be with him.

I couldn't see that his behavior was unacceptable. He would share stories about his ex-girlfriend, about how he caught her cheating on him so it was hard for him to trust girls. When he called me a few days later, I thought about that and assured him that I wasn't like those other girlfriends. I wouldn't cheat on him. I took him back and he was ok, for a few days. I had gotten to the point I was with him more than I was at home. I hadn't yet spent the night with him but I was coming in later and later and after school, I would get over there as quick as I could. He would walk me back home at night and I would come up the back stairs to sneak into the house. The hitting escalated. Once, I had come over to his house and he started accusing me of being with someone else almost as soon as I walked in the door. I was really getting tired of his accusations. He was threatening to choke me. I remember I was backed into the corner of his room near the window and the radiator. I was looking out the window with my elbow resting on the window pane, with my hand holding me head. I told him to just go ahead and choke me then. He grabbed me around my neck and I didn't say a word. The next thing I knew, I was on the floor and he was standing over me. I had felt a burning sensation going down my back but I didn't realize that I had began to loose consciousness and was sliding down the radiator. I woke up gasping for breath and he was standing over me saying "get up" but he had his hands in fists. I got up as quick as I could, amazed that he had choked me into unconsciousness. He had backed up and was looking at me, but I was bewildered. I grabbed my coat and ran out of the room, down the stairs and went home. He called a few days later and said how sorry he was and I went right back to him. I was afraid, but I was tired of the chaos. I was stuck and didn't know how to get out of this relationship.

Eventually I dropped out of school. I didn't tell my grandmother I wasn't going but I know she eventually was notified. My son was in daycare and on weekends, he would be with his grandmother. One day his grandmother called me and told me that she had some papers that I needed to sign so she could get health insurance for my son. She asked me which address she should use. I was spending so much time with my boyfriend, I gave her his address. She came over to my grandmother's house one day when I was home alone and showed me a letter of some sort. She told me that she needed my signature so that my son would have insurance coverage in her name.

I signed the paper and she told me she would take care of the whole thing. I was so naïve that I believed her. Later on I would realize that I had just signed away my parental rights. Reading the letter really didn't cross my mind. After this, I began spending the night at his house a few days during the week. One day, after I hadn't come home for a few days, my grandmother came to his house along with her cousin who happened to be a police officer. He and I were in his room in bed when we heard voices. When I realized it was my grandmother, I jumped up and put on some clothes. His father came to the door of his room and told us that she wanted to talk to us. We came out of the room, sat down and she asked me if he was keeping me there against my will. I told her no and he told her that if I wanted to go home, he had no problem with it. He was constantly smacking me by this time but I didn't really bruise so it didn't show. I would have bumps and lumps but no bruising. I figured that if I didn't have bruises, I wasn't being "abused". Some victims use this excuse to justify the abuse. They also tend to blame themselves. I told myself that I didn't want to make him feel like I wanted to be with anyone else so I stopped looking and interacting with the opposite sex. My grandmother's cousin and his father knew each other growing up so in the midst of this visit, they began talking. His dad told the officer he had heard us arguing but never witnessed any hitting or saw any evidence, (bruises). I told my grandmother I would be home that night because he had to go to church so she left with her cousin and I came home later that evening. I didn't know how she felt after leaving without me, but because I am now a parent and grandparent, I can imagine that her heart was torn because she knew I was in trouble.

I came home and thus began the pattern of me going to his house, staying until he had church and then coming home until Sunday when I would go back. He was getting worse. He had even began accusing me of being with members of my own family. I got to the point to where I wouldn't even go downstairs to visit my uncle or hang out on the porch when family was over. He had me under complete control. Soon I was going to church with him. I still loved him and wanted to be with him, but I was really tired of all the arguing. I guess I had had enough of it one day because I had planned on going to church with him one night but an argument ensued. He was coming to pick me up from my house so I got dressed in this nice skirt and a silk blouse and some heels that he had bought me. When he came and rang the bell, I came down the stairs. He immediately started an argument about how short my skirt was. I was upset because I thought I looked cute and really wanted to go with him and all he could do was yell about my skirt. He told me to go upstairs and change and I was refusing to. He went to push me back in the hallway and I began to swing. I think I hit him in the face because he was holding one arm up while trying to push me up the stairs. My grandmother was sitting in her front room and she must have heard the commotion and came running down the stairs yelling to him "get off her". He was yelling, "She is hitting me!" Finally, my grandmother had us separated and told him to just leave. He was saying he didn't do anything but ask me to change my skirt and I hit him first. Of course I was yelling but she finally got him to leave and got me upstairs. I finally went to my room to quiet down. We made up soon and I was back going to his house spending time over there again.

I became pregnant again sometime in the beginning of 1985. I told him and he began treating me kinder. I was happy because I thought that he had finally changed. I stopped spending the night at his house as often when I got further along, he then began spending time at my house. He had talked to my grandmother and assured her that he loved me and would take care of me and the baby. My family even threw me a baby

48

shower at my grandmother's house. It was a big party and he was right there in the mix. He bought me maternity clothes and everything. I went into labor on August 12th. I think it was during the early evening. I was at home, I think, and somehow got to the hospital. I remember he had gotten to the hospital but I wasn't in the final stage of labor. It was too early for the baby to come but my contractions were getting stronger and my water had broken after some time.

I guess I had been in labor for a few hours and he told me he would go home and get some things and come back soon. Sometime close to midnight, my contractions were coming faster but I didn't want to start pushing because he hadn't come back yet. I was in pain and uncooperative and they finally told me that I couldn't wait because the baby was coming. So I was wheeled into the delivery room and had the baby all by myself. After I delivered a 4lb 12oz baby boy and was in the stirrups waiting for them to finish cleaning him up, guess who strolls into the delivery room with shades and a big grin on his face. I was happy he made it, but would rather he had been there earlier. I realized later that he was high as a kite! He walked right past me to go see our son.

They didn't let me hold him right away and the nurse finally came and told me that he was going to NICU because he was so small. They said he was fine but he needed help breathing, so they were going to put him in an incubator and they would let me see him before they took him. I cried. While I was in the recovery room, they brought him in for me to see. He was beautiful, but tiny and had a plastic container like thing over his head. They had shaved off a tiny patch of hair on the side and had a needle in his scalp. They told me that he was too small to put an IV in his arm so they had to put it there. I was heart broken. My boyfriend was there and I remember him talking to me, but I was saddened because I couldn't hold him. We were finally able to go visit him, and at first neither of us knew what to do. I remember him crying when he first looked at the baby because they had taken blood samples from his feet and was hooked up to all these machines. The day I was released from the hospital, I had to go home without my baby. I was upset but there was nothing I could do about it. So, I left the hospital, but visited as much as I could. The hospital was right around the corner from my house. Sometimes he and I went together and would go to my house afterwards. He would stay for a few hours, but when it got late, my grandmother told him he had to leave. I remember my grandmother came into my room later that night and took my baby out of the crib and held him up to her.

I could see her smile as she looked at him. She kissed him and put him back down in the crib. She told me good night and left the room and I felt at ease. I believed it was going to be ok. Little did I know it would get worse.

For a few weeks, he would visit and stay for a while then go home. He was of course on his best behavior at my house. He soon suggested that we get a place of our own. I was ecstatic of course, because I figured we could be on our own and he would realize that I really loved him and we could be a nice little family. So he arranged for us to move into a three room apartment not too far from my grandmother's house. We got a few dishes and housewares from Woolworth's downtown. We got the baby crib over to the new apartment and I began the task of setting up our new home. Our bedroom was blue and we had a bed, a television on a crate and the crib in our room. I think the apartment was furnished but we had a couch and a kitchen table with some old chairs. I think our son was almost 2 months by this time. He was still tiny. I stayed inside the apartment because he didn't want me going anywhere with our son. He brought home groceries and I cooked and cleaned. There wasn't a lot of cleaning to do because we didn't have much. I really wasn't happy because he went right back to yelling at me. I was stuck in the house and overwhelmed with loneliness and a new baby.

One day, a man came to our door. I think it was the landlord, but I remember telling him that my boyfriend wasn't home. Whatever he wanted he had to wait until he came back to speak to him. When he finally got home, he started in on me. I don't remember how he knew, but when he found out about the man coming over, he got worse. The hitting started out in the kitchen and I eventually got away and ran to the bedroom. I ended up hiding under the crib because I was terrified. The baby was asleep but I had just enough room to slide under there so he wouldn't be able to hit me. I was begging for him to please leave me alone. I was promising to do whatever he wanted if he stopped hitting me. He kept telling me to get from under the crib but I refused to unless he promised to stop hitting me. Eventually he said he wouldn't hit me again and backed away from the crib. I was able to get from under it and ran to the front room and balled up on the couch. I felt hopeless. He came into the front room and spoke to me but that was it. Then he left. He must have come back later in the evening. I don't remember anything else, but me being there alone and the next day or so and my grandmother knocking on my door. She had come over to check on me and I guess I broke down and told her everything because the next thing I know, I am taking a bag full of clothes and my son and we were leaving that apartment and going back to her house.

I felt so lost and hopeless. I was running on automatic because I had withdrawn so deeply into myself. By the fall, my grandmother and mother had arranged for me to go to Ft. Lewis, Washington where my mother was stationed at the time. So I got a few things and prepared to go. I didn't tell anyone outside of my family and the day I was to fly, I went to pick up my oldest son from daycare and got on a plane to fly across the country. It was a relief but I really was unsure of the whole idea. My mother had been gone for a few years and I didn't know how I would feel about living with her again. She had gotten married to a man who had come to live on Custer for a while when she was transferring to Washington state. So, I had met him, but I didn't know him well. I landed in Seattle in the early evening and when I got off the plane, I was happy to see my mom. We hugged and she had some friends with her that she told me to stay with while she went to get my luggage.

Soon she came back with an officer and she took my oldest son and the officer proceeded to arrest me. I had no idea what was going on but it was later explained that my oldest son's grandmother got wind of where I was and had produced papers showing that she had custody of my son and I was being charged with kidnapping. She had flown to Seattle and took my son back to New Jersey. I was flabbergasted and I felt helpless. I didn't want to cry because as I was being taken into custody, I didn't want to look afraid. I knew how people were in jail and I had no intention of being some big girls' play toy. I was booked and strip searched, finger printed and photographed. I felt humiliated. I wanted my mom but she had to leave to straighten out the mess and her friends had my other son. After a few hours, dressed in a yellow jumpsuit with yellow plastic slippers on my feet, I was placed in a cell with about four bunks. It was crowded so I had a mattress that I had to place between two of the bunks on the floor to sleep. One girl asked me what I was in for and I said "kidnapping". She said to me, "you look to young to be in here." I felt a little better because she was telling me that nobody would mess with me. So I laid on my mat and went to sleep.

I was sleeping as peacefully as I could until I was awakened by lots of noise. I opened my eyes and looked up to see a girl from a top bunk leap over onto the other bunk and start beating the girl that was lying there. I was so scared that I slid my mattress under the far bunk and stayed there for a few minutes until the guards came in to calm everything down. I was able to make a phone call to my grandfather's house and talk to my sisters and everyone. Even though, I only stayed in that cell for an entire weekend, it felt like I was in there for years. I was finally let go that Monday evening. I was in Seattle and I had no idea what to do. When I was able to call my mom to get ready to go home, she told me to stay inside the building and wait until she got there. So I stood in the lobby of the building. It was dark outside and nobody was around.

Then a white girl who was in the cell with me came into the lobby. She smiled at me and I thought she was friendly until she said, "If I see you on the streets, I'm gonna make my dog bite your throat." Then she walked out the door. I was petrified! I hadn't done a thing to her but I will never forget her words. Finally, my mother arrived. My oldest son was already back in New Jersey and my youngest son was there with my mother's husband. She lived in a little town called Tacoma that was right outside of the military post. While the part of Seattle I was in was all lit up with bright lights, Tacoma was a dark little town. She pulled up to her house which was on the corner across from a horse ranch and right outside of the back of post.

There was absolutely nothing in her neighborhood and it was cold. She had a small house that didn't have a lot of furniture. There were two bedrooms, a small living area and kitchenette. I got settled in and went to sleep. The next day she told me how to get around by bus. She told me that I would be able to see Mt. Ranier if I took a walk around the neighborhood. There wasn't much to do in the area. I remember taking the bus to the little shopping plaza and I saw the mountain. It was snow covered and beautiful. She told me that her friends went to church and if I wanted I could go with them. A day or so later, we went to dinner at her friend's home and there was another couple that was there.

They had a little boy and they went to the same church. They told me they were trying to get my mom to come to church but she never attended. One day, I started to write a letter to my boyfriend. I hadn't finished it and left it on the dresser in my room. Later on that evening, I saw that my mother had written across the bottom of the letter, "don't do it Sandra." So I never finished the letter. She was looking out for me and I realized I needed to be away from him. I started attending Bible study and Sunday morning worship. The church was called Altheimer Memorial COGIC. I met so many people there who were encouraging and supportive. In fact, there was a young girl who attended that would grow up and become the first winner of BET's Sunday Best! Her parents were stationed at Ft. Lewis and we were invited to their home for dinner. The members of that church talked to me a lot about God and prayed for me. I enjoyed listening to the pastor preach. There was one older lady, I think she was a missionary, and she would even call me on the phone. I had a lot of questions. I wasn't sure if I was saved and when I told her about what happened when I went to church with my best friend years ago, she said that I had to pray for the gift of the Holy Ghost and then I would be saved. I remember there was some sort of revival service and in the middle of the service, the Spirit of God started moving and the next thing I knew, I was engulfed with this feeling of joy and I started jumping around. I felt myself moving around but I ended up hitting one of the ushers and knocking off her glasses. I went up for prayer and the preacher laid hands on me. I was at peace, but soon started having problems. It started out when I was at home I thought by myself one day. I was in the kitchen making bottles when all of a sudden, I felt someone touch my arm. I didn't realize my mother's husband was home but he was in his room with the door closed. I screamed and ran outside. He came running out the door asking me what was wrong. I was crying and it was then that he told me that there was a ghost in the house. I went back into my room and I didn't come out again. My mother finally came home and told me that the ghost was not scary, he just wanted to let me know he was here. I tried not to stay there after that. I would go down the street and stay all day at her friend's house.

I had began having nightmares and had trouble sleeping. I would wake up screaming and she would have to come in and sleep with me. It was during one of these times that she and I began talking and I started telling her all the things that happened to me when I was growing up. I would lay in her arms with my son wrapped up between us in this big sleeping bag and she would listen and then tell me what why she joined the military. Those were the closest moments she and I spent together and I then understood how much she loved me. It got to a point that I was emotionally coming apart. I wasn't sleeping and didn't like staying at the house by myself. She took me to her job once and introduced me to some people in her unit. There was some sort of function going on and there was a young man who was talking to her. She had introduced us but I was afraid of him. I didn't stay long at the function and finally she took me to one of the barracks of her friend and told me to go to sleep and she would be back to get me. I tried sleeping but I kept hearing voices and I truly thought I was going crazy. Then there was a knock on the door and when I opened it, the guy my mother introduced me to was standing there asking if I wanted to go for a walk. He seemed to be very nice but I just wasn't in my right mind. Finally, I called my mom and she sent me to her friend's house because she couldn't leave me alone.

I remember on the bus home, I started talking to God. I didn't know how to pray but I just started crying out for help deep in my soul. As I rode past Mt. Ranier, I remember looking at it and believing that if God could make such a magnificent mountain as that, He must be real and I believed that He had to have heard my cry. I still was having trouble. I was at Bible study one evening and we were holding class in one of the downstairs rooms at the church. There was a young man that I thought was very cute and he would speak to me on occasion. Well during the service, I was sitting in a pew and I heard my boyfriend call my name. I was afraid and I began looking around. I happened to look in the back of the room and I thought that I saw him sitting back there looking scary. I thought I was going insane. All of a sudden, he was leaning over in the pew hiding his face and sitting back laughing at me. I was shaking and someone must have come over and began talking to me to get me to calm down. The next thing I remember people began praying over me and I ended up going to the front of the room. The preacher laid hands on me and then I ended up on the floor talking some sort of gibberish. The people were praying and talking over me. I didn't know what was going on. After it was all over, I remember the missionary began talking to me and telling me that whenever I began seeing things like that to start praying and say the blood of Jesus. Then she gave me a Bible. I went to my mom's friend house that night because she was in the field so she wouldn't be home. My mother's friend sat and talked with me about the Bible for hours. She had crosses up in her front room and Bibles and scripture pictures everywhere. Finally, it was time to go to sleep and she covered me up on the couch and turned out the lights.

It was dark in the room and I tried to sleep. I kept tossing and turning. Soon though, my eyes began closing. Then the nightmares started and I began calling on Jesus. I had heard a song by Vanessa Bell Armstrong called Peace Be Still and all of a sudden, I heard a voice in my head. I had calmed down, but then I felt my heart begin to flutter. I was afraid for a moment then I heard the Spirit of God say to me in a sing song voice, "I want to touch your heart." He kept saying it over and over and soon I was calm. My mind was still afraid and I was unsure if it was God or the devil until His voice spoke saying, "Satan can't touch you" over and over again. It was dark in the room but in my mind's eye, the light of God was all over me. I began crying and felt a deep sense of relief. I slept sounder than I had in weeks. When I woke up the next day, I felt so much better. I was able to stay at the house and I began devouring the Bible. I had so many questions and the people at the church talked to me about every question I had. I had even exchanged numbers with the young man and we began having phone conversations. Down the road from the horse ranch was a payphone. I would walk across the street to stand at the fence and the horses would come up to me. Then I would go to the payphone to call him. I thought I had fallen in love and told him so. I told him I wanted to marry him. He said if God's will was for us to marry we would get married. He was very kind and respectful. He listened to me and I had never felt that before. We never went out but we would see each other two or three times a week at church and talk on the phone.

Everything was going much better. I wasn't even thinking about my baby's father. I thought I would stay in Washington state forever but after about three months, my mother told me that she had to PCS. She was leaving Washington and asked me if I wanted to stay. Her friends told me I was more than welcome to stay with them and she told me that I could go to school there. Even though I was happier than I had been in a long time, I was afraid to be so far from my family. Looking back, things would be a lot different if I had stayed, but it was not to be so. My grandmother found out and I remember that she was not having me stay all the way on the west coast. So after a few months, I was back in New Jersey. My son was now nine months. When I got back to New Jersey the first thing I did was call my boyfriend, of course. He immediately came to my grandmother's home to see us. He was crying when he saw his son. I felt bad about leaving him but I knew I had to. He told me how sorry he was about hurting me and he would never put a hand on me. I still had deep feelings for him. We talked on the phone often.

It took a few months for me to trust him enough to spend time with him but after a while I would go and visit him. We didn't have sex right away because I was still unsure. Plus, I didn't want to get pregnant. He never wanted to use birth control, he used the old, "it doesn't feel real to me" line so I never used condoms. I was taking birth control pills for a while but I often forgot. I did talk him into letting me use a diaphragm when we started having sex again. That only worked for a little while. So sometime in the summer of 1986, I became pregnant again. He was staying at someone's house near the church he played the organ for because his dad moved from Newark to East Orange which was further away. We were off and on involved. My family was telling me to leave him alone but I thought I was still in love with him. Then one day I decided to ask him to marry me. I bought a bottle of his favorite cologne, a card and wrote him a note and left it in his mail box. I went home and he called me soon after. We met and went to his house where he was living in a room in the basement. He had a candlelight dinner prepared on a crate table that he set up. His room was finished but it was still a basement and we had to go through the dusty part to get to his room.

We began to eat and talk. He was wearing a brown silk tie. He leaned over and kissed me and I remember suddenly, that tie caught fire from the candle. It was only a little burn that left a small hole but we laughed about it for a while. We went to get a cheap wedding band from downtown and an off white lace dress for me and one Sunday morning, his pastor announced that we were going to be married at the morning service. Everyone was cheering and clapping! We had gotten the license and two of the women who I had began to talk to helped me get dressed. I still had my jheri curl shag hair style and I had borrowed some pearls from someone. His mother and one of his sisters came to the church that day. I hadn't told my family at all. When it was time for the ceremony to start, I walked out from the back and he was standing at the altar with a white tux. When I got in front of him, I began singing "Endless Love" by Lionel Richie and Diana Ross and when I looked at him, he had tears running down his face. I was happy and thought we were going to be just fine. We went to his place and there was a small celebration with the people he was living with.

One of his older brothers was living there at the time and I remember they had some bottles of Champale. We toasted and went to one of the rooms on the main floor. We were in the room and everything was going good, but later we ended up arguing. He was in my face cussing at me and he ended up telling me to go home. I think he was afraid to hit me while I was pregnant. So I went back to my grandmother's house. A few days later, she looked at me and said, "So you're married huh?" I felt shame but answered her yes. That was all that was spoken about it. We lived separately for a while. At some point, my grandad and granny ended up buying a two story house in the Vailsburg section of Newark which was closer to East Orange where his father lived. By this time, it was the two of us and two children. My daughter was born March 9, 1987. I stayed with him off and on wherever he was living, which wasn't always a decent place. We stayed a few times with his father, but it didn't last long because there was really no room. His older sister was living with his dad at that time. I ended up moving back to my grandad's house eventually. He wasn't allowed to live there with me. In fact, at that time, my grandfather wouldn't even allow him on the front porch because we would argue so much. I know a few times, my grandad came out on the porch and told him to get out. Everyone was still telling me to leave him alone but I wasn't listening. We ended up in a homeless shelter sometime in 1988 while I was pregnant with my third child by him. There was a hotel in downtown Newark where the city would pay for vouchers for welfare recipients to stay. They provided money to pay for food from the restaurant at the hotel. We would get dressed to go to church every Sunday. I was able to buy nice dresses and clothes for myself and the children and he always had someone giving him suits that he would wear every Sunday. Imagine us dressed in our Sunday best coming out of a homeless hotel. Some of his friends teased him whenever we were coming or going, talking about how sharp he was.

The reason he couldn't keep a steady place to live was because by this time, he was abusing crack. He was paid weekly by the church he was playing, for so at times he didn't have rent money. I was getting welfare and since we were married, he was added to the case. So I had food stamps to buy formula and milk and he bought pampers but the rest of his money went to drugs. In fact, out of all the adults in the hotel, except for myself and I think one or two other adults, were using drugs of some sort. This was during the time when crack cocaine addiction was pandemic in most inner cities across the country. He was at a different church by now, and had a weekly income. He was hitting me still and I had completely withdrawn from interacting with anyone but my children and him. He was using and there were times when he would bring one or two people into the room and close the bathroom door to use. There was only one room and the children slept on a roll away bed. There was a dresser and a television along with a queen bed in the room and we had a hotplate, which was really prohibited, but just about everyone had one. On May 9, 1988, I went into labor and went to St. Michael's hospital. I gave birth to a baby girl. While in the hospital, we talked to a social worker and decided to place our youngest daughter temporarily in foster care. We had been in the shelter for a few months and I really didn't want to bring the new baby into that hotel. I was completely hopeless and things were really bad between us. The social worker brought the paperwork to have her placed into foster care until we were able to get on our feet. I was under the impression that because this was voluntary, as soon as we got out of the hotel, we could get her back. This turned out not to be the case though. So, the day when I went home, I was able to spend my last few moments with her. I went to our room and once I was settled, he left. I believe my grandmother had our son during my hospital stay. My oldest daughter had a godmother from the church who would take her for weekends. She attended the church he was going. She took a liking to me after we got married and when I had my oldest daughter, she bought her so many clothes and things that she really didn't want for anything. While we were in the shelter, she would bring things to us. My grandmother also came to the hotel often once she found out where we were. She worked downtown at the US Post Office and during some of our hard times, I would go borrow money from her. I don't even remember how the conversation started but when it was time to sign the foster care papers, we signed them and left our child at the hospital. When I got back to the hotel, I was emotionally numb and didn't have any outlet to talk about what was going on. I was in my room a few days later and I don't even remember if my children were with me but I remember laying in that bed crying and moaning because I wanted my baby. I was in deep despair and I am unsure of how long it lasted. Soon afterwards, he began hitting me again. His drug use was really extreme by this time. One evening after an argument, he left the room. I assumed he was somewhere copping a hit. Someone knocked on my door a few hours later. I looked through the peephole and noticed it was a guy that lived on our floor. He and his wife and family were staying a few doors down. They seemed nice and his wife sometimes talked to me when we were downstairs in the restaurant. The guy told me that he needed to talk to me. I was afraid because I didn't want my husband to get mad but he assured me that my husband knew that he was coming to talk to me. So he came in and sat on the corner of the bed while I sat on the roll away bed closer to the door with my children lying there. He told me that my husband had stolen some money or drugs from him. He told me that he didn't appreciate being stolen from and he had him in his room and he wasn't going to let him out until he talked to me. He told me that he knew he was hitting me and told me that if he ever put his hand on me again other than to hug me or love on me to let him know and he would whoop his ass. I was afraid because I thought he was beat up bad. The guy told me that he did hit him, but my husband had promised to pay him back the next time he got paid. The guy told me that he would be watching and listening and all I had to do was let him know if my husband hurt me. A few hours later, my husband came back into the room looking a little roughed up and anxious. He asked me if the guy had come into the room. I told him yes. When he asked me if he touched me, I said no. He then told me that the guy had told him he would rape me if he didn't pay him back. He had some other guys hold him back in the room while he came to talk to me. I kept telling him that he didn't touch me and he finally believed me. He didn't hit me much after that, but the drug use worsened. Another incident took place a while later. He had a cousin who was also living in the hotel. Sometimes, I would have her kids and my kids in the room while the two of them went to smoke. There were a few other people he would go smoke with or bring to our room. One day, I went upstairs to his cousin's room and she had a few of the kids there while they went off to smoke. I think someone called the room and I found out that one of the ladies was on the way to the emergency room. She was with them smoking and I remember there was a commotion in the hallway. I heard the sirens and remembered going to the window to look out and I saw her laid out on the stretcher. I believe she died of heart failure due to the drugs. I remember looking down on her from the window, feeling sad and for the life of me, I couldn't figure out how I ended up in this condition.

We stayed in the hotel for a few more months. I don't even recall how many, but I know we stayed in that hotel more than once. A little while after my second daughter was born we found a place. We were given vouchers for furniture and moved into a nice little two room place. We even had a birthday party for our oldest daughter while living there. She was about 2 or three. My grandmother had come over and so had his mother and her godmother. It was a nice little gathering. At some point, we began trying to get our daughter back but the social worker began telling us that we needed to take parenting classes and had to be tested by a psychiatrist. We didn't think we needed them because we had voluntarily placed our daughter in foster care. We ended up asking my grandmother if she would take her. She was still working at the time but she did go to court with us to see if the judge would give her custody of our daughter but they denied her. We had been tested and the results showed that I was the aggressive and controlling parent and my husband was passive and only agreed to place her in foster care because I was insisting on it. We got to see her two times during the whole process. The last time was when she was almost a year and a half old. We sat in the reception area and I think they were testing us because a lady came in with a baby and I didn't realize that the baby she was holding was mine. They called us into the office in the back and when the social worker brought the baby to us, I was in shock. I think that I was so numb to what my situation was that I don't remember exactly what was going on. We were told that our baby had already bonded with the adoptive parent and because of that, it was best that she stayed with her. Our rights were terminated and we were not allowed to have contact with her. That literally just left a bigger hole in my heart and it was compounded by the fact that I had lost custody of my oldest son and my husband was a drug addict who still physically abused me. I became pregnant soon after we moved into the new apartment and decided to go to a planned parenthood clinic downtown near our house. I arranged to have another abortion. I went through the procedure alone and was completely distraught. While there, I spoke to a woman who was a counselor. After I had the procedure, I began going to the clinic regularly to talk to this woman. She was very kind and understanding. I would spend at least an hour each time I came to her office. I was able to talk freely about how I felt and she was very supportive. She began telling me about Narcotics Anonymous meetings for people who had loved ones that were addicted to drugs and encouraged me to go. I was such a wreck emotionally, but after talking to her, I began feeling such relief. At our apartment, we had a pattern where my husband would come from church on a Sunday, get high, sit up all night, crash when the morning came and get up later feeling bad. Because we were still receiving food stamps we had food in the house most times. He started selling some of them eventually. I would go to the grocery store to get food and leave him with the kids. One time, he convinced me to take him and leave the kids alone. The store wasn't far away but we put the television on in their room and left them in there. When we got back, they had gotten out of the room and had detergent and baby powder everywhere and diapers were all over the floor. Their room was a mess with clothes and the little bit of toys they had were everywhere. I was so upset and he promised that we would never leave them like that again. God truly had his hand on us. I know that could have turned out a lot worse than it did.

We eventually were put out of that apartment and ended up staying with my grandmother. I became pregnant again and had another boy in November 1989. I remember I was hiding my pregnancy, or so I thought, by dressing in big clothes. My water had broken one evening, I think it was right after Thanksgiving and I didn't say anything for a while. Finally, early the next morning, I had to go tell my grandmother because I was in pain. I told her that I needed to go to the hospital. When I told her I was pregnant, she said, "I know" and drove me to the hospital. I brought this baby home and we soon moved into another apartment not too far from my grandmother's. My husband had begun playing at a different church. The pattern was that he would start playing at a church, then when they found out that he was using drugs they would try and give his money to me. That would only work while we were in their presence. As soon as we got home, most times after whoever took us home after a stop at the grocery store, he would take the money and go use it up. We would have food for a few days but when we ran out, the money was gone so I would have to go borrow and beg for food from people we knew. We stayed in this apartment for a longer time because we were getting rental assistance. His drug use continued and I was trying hard to keep us stable but there were times when he would threaten me if I didn't give him "his" money. I couldn't leave it in my purse because he would steal it when he thought I was asleep. I would hide it in the food boxes, in the ceiling tiles, in the refrigerator but none of that worked. There were times when I would have to fight to keep him from taking the food and rent money. On Sundays, we would go to the store to buy dinner and I would come home and cook. He would immediately go out and get high. He would come home at two in the morning and I would then cook his dinner. Then one night, he went out to get high after church and as usual, he came in after midnight. I went into the kitchen and began cooking him pork chops. While I was at the stove, he came into the house and sat on our bed which was close to the kitchen, and began telling me that God had saved his life. He began telling me that he was going into this building to buy drugs and he was robbed in the stairwell. He said that the guys had choked him until he passed out and when he got up, God told him to go home. He always went to buy drugs in the suit he wore to church and people would call him "Preach" and he would laugh. He also wore shades all the time to hide his glassy eyes. That night after he finished telling me the story, he took off his shades. His eyes were red. They weren't the high red eyes, his eyes were bright blood red. He also had bruises on his neck. I started crying and we immediately started praying. He kept saying that God saved his life and for a while, he didn't use drugs. That incident scared him but he was soon back to using. We began attending another church soon called Refuge Tabernacle. It was a small church and there was a daycare on one side of the church. They had a church bus and would come pick us up. Before long, the drug abuse began to have an effect again. He would sometimes get paid for a whole day right after morning service and then not show up for the evening service. The pastor eventually found out what was going on and tried to help by holding some of his pay and taking us grocery shopping, but of course it didn't last long. It got back to where we couldn't stay in the apartment. When we were getting ready to be evicted, he sent me out to call the pastor of and he came over to the house. We were sitting in the front room and he asked me what I wanted to do. Of course my husband began talking but for the first time, someone was asking me about my situation. He told my husband to go into the kitchen because he wanted to talk to me. I didn't know what I wanted to do but I was so exhausted physically and emotionally by then, it didn't dawn on me that I didn't have to put up with the treatment he gave me. But that was the first time someone showed any concern about me and my feelings. So we called my father in law and asked if we could stay there. He said yes and the pastor drove us with all we could pile into his car to East Orange. We began living with my husband's father. His sister had gotten married and moved out so there was room for us to stay there. His father had a room in the back of the house and worked all day. So, during the day, it was just us. When his father came home in the evening, he would do the same thing everyday. He would cook his dinner, make his lemonade and then he would go in his room to watch television. Then we wouldn't see him for the rest of the night. It was often during these times that more abuse would take place. My husband would close the door to the kitchen. The living room was right next to the empty bedroom that we slept on the floor in. I remember one night, after his dad had gone to bed, we had a bad argument. It was late and the kids were on the floor on blankets. I think my next to the youngest was laying in the carrier in the other room as well. I remember that he was threatening to kill me. He had gotten a knife from the kitchen and was sitting on the couch. He had just gotten up off of the chair where he had been hitting me upside my head. I remember that I was covering my head and was pleading with him to stop. He sat on that couch and had the knife in his hand threatening to stab me. I kept promising him I would do anything if he would just put the knife down. He continued to sit there and I watched him until he finally fell asleep. I slept as best as I could and the kids somehow remained quiet.

The next morning, he didn't speak to me. His dad had gone off to work and he left sometime early in the day. I was so lost and confused. I didn't know what to do so I went into the kitchen and sat at the table. I was crying and looking out of the window. I began telling God how tired and hurt I was. Then I heard his voice say "Get up and leave." I thought to myself, "I don't have anywhere to go." He told me to call my pastor. I called him and told him I needed to get out of that house. He picked me up and I left with my four kids and was pregnant with my last child who would be born in March of 1992. When I found out I was pregnant with this child, I tried to abort it. I remember going to the clinic and they told me I was too far along to abort. So when I left the clinic I was crying and praying. I remember walking up the street to the bus stop to go home and looking up into the sky. It was clear and I remember asking God, "How am I going to make it with another child?" I heard His voice reply, "I will take care of you, trust me". When He spoke that day, I decided to trust Him but I had no idea what I would have to go through. That day at my father in law's house, sitting in the kitchen, God spoke again. This time, I didn't hesitate to make that call. My pastor took me back to my grandfather to live. I became a member of that church and I faithfully attended for about 4 years. There was a bus that would come pick me up during the week for service and on Sunday morning. I began reading my Bible often and praying more and more. I didn't understand but God was drawing me closer to Him and strengthening me. I remember we had a class that someone spoke about abortions. We were in the dining area and watched a film about what happens during abortions. I remember sitting in the dark watching it and I began crying because the film was saying that although abortion is a sin, God can forgive women who have them and I realized that God didn't hate me, but He loved me in spite of what I had done. I began get close to the members of that church and began looking to my pastor as a father figure. A little over a month after my last child was born in March of 1992, while we were still living with my grandfather, my granny had gotten sick. She had stopped working by this time and was a full blown alcoholic. My grandad was still working for the liquor company and people had been staying at the house that he was finally able to buy off and on for years. Two of my sisters had graduated from high school while they were living there and one attended college for a short while. Just after my second youngest sister finished one semester of college, my mother had taken the three of them to live with her in Germany where she was stationed. It was a two story house. There was a partially finished basement and attic. By the time I got back to that house, the only person living there was my grandfather's brother. By this time, Granny was so sick, she was relegated to stay downstairs in the den in a hospital bed because she couldn't get up the stairs. She would get drunk on Christian Brother's Brandy and milk and commence to yelling and cussing everybody out from her "throne" on the side of the hospital bed, smoking her Newport cigarettes. I remember her being so sick and she kept calling me to come do stuff for her. After I gave birth to my youngest child, I had to tell her that I couldn't come downstairs because I was still recovering. When I was finally able to get up and down the stairs, she began having trouble going to the bathroom so I had to help her get up and get on the portable pot in the den. I was playing nursemaid to her and taking care of my kids. Two of them were in school up the street so I would take them to school in the morning and spend my day changing diapers for my babies and her. I was miserable. One night, mid - April of 1992, she was so sick that she asked me to call the ambulance. I told my grandfather who had gotten home after a long day at work and he waited upstairs while the paramedics came in and put her on a stretcher. I watched as they carried her to the ambulance and remember thinking that was going to be the last time I saw her alive. Little did I know death was coming but not the way I thought. She stayed in the hospital for a week or so. I called her every day and my grandad went up there once or twice. I was relieved because she wasn't calling my name all day and night. My great uncle, Grandad's younger brother who was staying there, was working the night shift and my grandad worked days so most of the time, it was me and the kids in the house. My grandad would get up early in the morning before I had to take my kids to school and my uncle would be home before I had to leave so he would watch the babies while I walked the older two up the street. During this time, my last three were all less than a year apart and none of them slept through the night so for about three years straight, I got no sleep at night. If the youngest woke up because he was hungry, he would start the next to the youngest crying and by the time I got them settled, my middle son would be up crying. I was a zombie by this time but I kept muddling along. That April night, I slept really hard. About two or three in the morning, I jumped up out of my sleep because I heard a loud bam and felt the house shake and I remember calling Jesus. I went right back to sleep and the babies didn't wake up any more that night. It was April 23, 1992. I remember because it was Granny's birthday and my oldest son was born on April 27th. I woke up again around 7:00 am because someone was calling my grandad's name in the driveway. The night before, he had come home and went straight up to his room. He told me he wasn't feeling well and he probably wasn't going to work in the morning. I was sitting in the chair in the front room watching television. The kids were all spread out on the floor and couches and the only light that was on was the lamp near me. I saw my grandfather and although it didn't dawn on me then, it seemed that there was a shadow surrounding him. So when I woke up to hear the guy who rode with my grandfather calling him from the driveway, I opened the window and told him that he wasn't feeling well and wouldn't be going to work. I thought nothing else about it and went back to sleep. About an hour later I finally woke up. By 8:00 am, my uncle would have been home. I hadn't heard him come in. I came out of the room and began going down the stairs.

The house had a staircase that turned and on the second landing there was a small hallway with the rooms next to each other. Coming out of the master bedroom where me and my kids slept, I had to turn toward the right and there was the bathroom and another room across from it where my grandad began sleeping. So I couldn't see into the room going down the stairs. I saw his slipper in the hall in front of the bathroom but I didn't think anything was wrong. When I got downstairs, I noticed that the screen door in the enclosed porch was opened. The front door to get into the house was locked. I thought that was strange but didn't pay any mind to it. It was still very quiet in the house. I thought the kids were still asleep. I went into the kitchen for a moment and then began walking back up the stairs. As I turned the landing, I was able to see into my grandad's room and saw him lying on the floor. I yelled for him and went into shake his foot then ran back down the stairs. I called my grandmother and my uncle but couldn't reach them. This was before cell phones were invented. I left messages at their job. Then I called Granny's son who lived in Virginia at the time. He answered and I told him what happened. He told me to go up and check his pulse. I was afraid but I ran up there to touch his neck. He had already begun to stiffen. I knew that he was already gone. I ran back down the stairs and wailed into the phone that he was dead. He told me to call the ambulance and not to touch anything until he got to there. I was in shock. I was all alone with my kids. I remember after I hung up the phone, I went outside to the neighbor's house to ask for help because I didn't know what else to do. She was upset but she didn't come to the house. I went back inside and called my pastor and he told me that he would be on the way. I was completely distraught. I don't even remember if the kids were crying. I was too afraid to go back upstairs. Within minutes the paramedics were there and not too long afterwards, my pastor arrived. I believe it was he who finally got the kids downstairs and began getting breakfast prepared for them. He was in the kitchen cooking and cleaning up while my relatives began to arrive. I don't remember who arrived next, but I remember eventually my grandmother, my great-uncle who lived there, my aunts and my uncle came to the house. I was still in the front room on the chair. My uncle went up to the bedroom while we were waiting for the coroner to arrive. My grandmother had arrived and was sitting near me and I believe one of my aunts was on the couch. We sat and waited and eventually the coroner brought his body downstairs wrapped in a sheet. As he was coming down, I remember looking up and everyone was crying. Soon everyone had begun gathering at the house. I introduced my pastor to my family because they were wondering who this man was in the kitchen cleaning up. He kept asking everyone if they needed anything. I think he even went shopping. The members of the church had already been dropping off food and gifts for my new baby. Almost all of my family had arrived by the evening but I was awaiting the most important person of all to come home. My mom and two of my sisters who were still overseas. She was the last one in the family to arrive at the house. A few days later when my mommy had finally arrived, I ran outside into her arms and immediately broke down crying. She took me back into the house and ushered me upstairs where I relished the comfort of her arms as I hadn't in a long time. I think one of my relatives were trying to help her comfort me but she told them to leave the room and I was able to lean on her as she soothed me. As we prepared for my grandfather's burial, I was in a daze. Family members were coming and going in and out of the house. When it was time to go to the wake, I was the last one to arrive at the funeral parlor because I had to wait until there was a car available for me and my kids. Everyone was already in the funeral parlor and people had begun coming out. While I was standing in the lobby of the funeral parlor, I noticed my great aunt whose house I used to clean standing next to a man in a wheel chair whom I didn't recognize. He was watching me but didn't say anything. I didn't go over to him because I had no idea who he was. I was talking to someone one after I went past him and the person told me it was my great uncle, the one who abused members of my family. I had learned he was very ill. He had been a tall, dark skinned man. The man I saw in the wheelchair was pale and almost emaciated. It was a shock to see him. I didn't speak to him, but headed into the room where my grandad's body was laying. He looked so peaceful. I remember holding up my middle son who would often go into his room and sit on the bed and snack on the candy that my grandad would keep in a can near his night stand. Whenever I couldn't find my son in the house when my grandad was home, I knew he was upstairs watching television with him eating his snacks. My son would often pretend to fight him and my grandfather would say, "Hey dude" and give him a "knuckle sandwich". As I stood there holding him he kept pointing to him saying "granddaddy"? I told him yes, that was granddaddy and I remember him waving good bye to him. It was then that I bent down and kissed my grandfather on the forehead. I watched as my grandmother came and knelt on the platform in front of the casket. She was patting his chest. I thought about how even though they both had lived apart for many years, there must have been a great love between them. The next day we had a Catholic funeral so the casket was closed. His side of the family attended this Catholic church, but they were not practicing Catholics that I know of. I remember his mother and aunt's funerals were held there. I remember looking up into the ceiling during the service because the ceilings were painted with stations of the cross. I remember I felt a sense of peace and trust in God that I hadn't felt before. I began crying and I forgot who was sitting next to me but they put their arm around me. I wasn't crying tears of sadness, but I was thanking God for getting me through the whole situation. We went back to the house and people were coming and going. I don't think Granny's son attended the funeral. He and I went to the hospital to tell her that he had passed the day he arrived. The next day or so, he began packing up things in the house saying that he was taking his mom back to Virginia with him and he was taking all of the furniture. There was a huge fight about it because he had gone through all of my grandad's belongings before we had the chance to mourn him. Although they

71

weren't together, my grandmother was still legally his wife and therefore, the rightful beneficiary to all of his assets. My grandmother was doing well. She still had the house on Custer and she worked for the post office. Granny was still in the hospital. Sometime during all of the arrivals of everyone else and the planning for the funeral, he was behind the scenes going through stuff in the house. After the service, I remember that my grandmother, mother, aunts and uncle were talking with him in the kitchen and an argument broke out. He wanted to start taking the furniture and take his mom back to Virginia with him and I remember him yelling, "Y'all ain't gonna leave my momma with nothing. She has the right to everything here." The grandchildren and cousins were in the front room. Everyone was telling him to just wait and everything would be taken care of. He wouldn't listen and I think a scuffle was about to take place and I heard my grandmother say, "Keith let him take the stuff. We don't need any of it." I remember that he kept telling me the whole time before the funeral not to let anyone go through my grandad's stuff. I wasn't mentally aware of how everything was going. Eventually, my family decided to let him take everything. The next day or so after the service, he rented a u haul and took every piece of furniture except the mattress and box spring and me and my kids belongings and drove it to Virginia with his mother. We watched as he cleared out the garage. My family was already distraught but my grandmother kept telling us that the stuff wasn't important. I think the worst thing was that he took my grandfather's coins and medals from when he was in the Korean war and that was the only thing my uncle said he wanted. Right after that we got word that our uncle, the one who had been the abuser and who was sick, had passed away as well. We had to prepare for another funeral. He had apparently been sick for a while and there were probably preparations made beforehand. The only thing I remember was that when we went to the funeral, his wife and family were sitting in front pew, my grandmother was next to her and the next 5-6 rows were empty and the rest of the family was seated far away from the front. I don't remember where the funeral was held, but you could feel how much tension was in the room. I remember looking at my aunt who still lived at home with granny at the time looked so angry and I don't think she stayed long. The whole service to me seemed surreal.

The next problem was what to do with me and my kids. I had been between my grandmother and grandad's house and back and forth with my husband for years. This time it was decided that I would move back to Custer Avenue on the first floor because my uncle and aunt would be moving into their own house soon. Until I was ready to move back to Custer, I slept on the floor in the room we were in because my great uncle was making plans to move to an apartment. I think it was closer to his job. He still worked nights so a few weeks after the funeral and everyone was about their own way, I was in the house alone most of the time. One night, I was having a fretful sleep. It was late and I dreamt that while I was tossing and turning, my grandfather came into the room and kissed me on my forehead. I saw him in his white thermal underwear he always had on. It was as if he was watching me toss and turn and when he kissed me, I opened my eyes and saw him smile and was able to go back to sleep peacefully. I felt that he was telling me good bye and that I would be alright. I stayed in the house for a few more days and finally, me and my five children went back to live with my grandmother. We didn't move downstairs onto the first floor because soon my aunt and uncle got divorced. All of us slept in one room on a bunk bed. I was still going to church often and trying to get on my feet. I enrolled into a certificate program for medical secretaries and even found a job at a nursing home for a short time. I began volunteering at the day care at my church because my youngest three were attending while the older two were in school. I was beginning to understand more about God during this time. I learned a lot about faith in God and studied His word more and more. I learned how to pray earnestly to God while here. I was a single parent trying to raise 4 boys and a girl with a lot of support from my church. I was active in the choir, usher board, Sunday school and Bible study. It was while attending this church I found my favorite scripture. I began talking with my pastor about some of the things I had gone through with my husband. He told me to read Psalms 139:14 and I began to believe it. I realized that I was beautiful and that God loved me. I began to understand that my husband didn't love me the way I deserved and was created to be loved. His abuse was what took the last bit of worth I had in myself. He still tried to get me to take him back. He would show up at the day care trying to convince me to come back to him. In fact, one day, I was at the day care and he showed up. My pastor told me to go into his office and he would deal with him. I heard him outside the door in the hallway of the daycare yelling, saying he knew I was there somewhere. He and I didn't live together again until I got to Texas. There were three church mothers who I talked to often and I was close with mostly all of the members. They had become just like family and my pastor had become a father figure. I spent a lot of time at church. By this time, my mother had returned from overseas and was preparing to build a house in Texas. She kept telling me to come to Texas but I didn't want to live with her. I wanted to stay connected to my church. I even began looking for an apartment nearby so I could get to church easily. I had begun taking courses at the local college and was really trying to get on my feet. I found out about an apartment right around the corner from the church one day while at the daycare center. I went to go look at it and then I went back to the daycare center. I remember talking to my Pastor and he told me to pray about it and if I trusted God, He would give me the desires of my heart. I remember going into the sanctuary and kneeling at the front and I prayed earnestly for God to let me get that apartment. I had enrolled into a surgical technician program and my plan was to finish, get an apartment and a car and get on my feet. I never got the apartment. I wasn't sure what my next move was. God was working behind the scenes though. Our church would host a large Christmas party every year and we would give out toys to people in the community and have dinner and sing. I really enjoyed those times. One year, there was a tragic accident that really shook us. The church was located on a main street between Newark and Irvington NJ. Two blocks up, there was a side street that the bus would turn after its last stop in Newark before heading to Irvington. It was a number street but there was nothing on it but a few warehouses. It was known as 'Hoe Strow" because prostitutes hung out here. There were addicts and dealers that hung out right next door in the abandoned building next to the sanctuary doors of the church and crime was rampant. But the community respected Pastor and they didn't give us too hard a time. The night of one particular Christmas party, there was a car accident in front of the church. We just heard this loud noise and when we all went outside, we saw the cars and a woman was on the ground with a head injury lying near the curb. Pastor was helping with the traffic and we were praying and trying to help. When it was cleared and we went back into the church, it was sad but we prayed and Pastor preached. We began singing and praising God. We took up an offering and gifts to give to the family. I believe the woman lost her child in the accident.

I first learned how to witness while I was a member at this church and we would go out and evangelize the community. We had some sidewalk services where we would sing and pray and pastor would preach. Some people would join us from the neighborhood and we would pass out tracts. The first time I went out to witness, I walked to where a crowd of people were standing and as soon as they saw me coming with my "sanctified skirt" you know the one that was denim and went past my knees, the crowd dispersed! I turned to look at my pastor and he laughed and told me to keep striving. I talked to a few more people. When we went back in, we all laughed about it more. Because I had been spending so much time at the daycare, my kids were always with me. The church bus would pick them up from school and drop them off and if we had service that evening, I was able to cook dinner and feed them. We would get dropped off at home by the van or one of the members. One day, all of my kids and some other kids were left at the church while the adults went out to do street witnessing. There was a boy who was about 14 that lived in the neighborhood and had become a regular visitor. He seemed to be helpful. He helped everyone and could often be found cleaning up or taking out trash. One night, we had a service at another church and we all rode the van. The kids were all in the back and this boy was sitting on the back row with the smaller children. We had a long service and traveling back, it was late at night so most of them were asleep. About two days later, I think one of the deaconess' called and I was told that this young boy had touched one of the other girls on that trip and she told them that he had touched them before at church. My daughter was one of the children he touched. I was distraught. I didn't understand how this could happen to my child. This boy had become close to my family and had even visited my home. I never imagined that this would happen while we were here. We were in church where I thought we would be safe. When I spoke to my pastor, he told me that he had gone to the boy's home and told him to stay away from the church. The boy's mother told him that she had problems with before and promised that he would never come back there again. An investigator talked to my daughter about the incident but I don't recall what happened afterwards. We continued there as members for a few years more. Then on June 24, 1995, a trial came that was worse than anything I ever imagined took place and it became the catalyst to move me from dependency on people to a total faith and dependency on God.

It was a Saturday afternoon. There was a Youth Department event at church and I was taking the bus to get there. My daughter had gone to Irvington with my aunt, who took the bus there to run errands just about every Saturday. My grandmother was home and the boys and I walked to Hawthorne Avenue to catch the Number 27 bus to the church which was right on the borderline of Newark and Irvington. The bus would let us off on the corner and we would walk the half block right to the church doors. It was a beautiful summer day and the walk to the bus stop was about 8 blocks away and we had to cross over a bridge that went over the highway. We walked to the bus stop to the corner of Hawthorne Avenue and Osborne Terrace. Several incidents happened there previously that were tragic. There were accidents there often because young guys would fly down the hill doing "donuts" right in the middle of the intersection. "Donuts" were the fad, kids in cars speeding and spinning out in an intersection. They were just joyriding, but some serious accidents had taken place. The accident before my son's had a baby ejected from the car that died at the scene. Because it was early afternoon, it was relatively safe during that time. So we got to the corner and were preparing to cross the street to catch the bus up the hill. The light was green for us and as we were getting ready to cross, I heard a horn blowing to my left. As I looked up, I saw a van approaching the intersection and realized that they were not slowing down. I had my four boys with me. My youngest was in my left arm, my middle son had my right hand, my second oldest son was holding his hand and my next to the youngest was on the end. We could see the bus coming up the street, but it was still a few blocks away. As I realized that the van wasn't going to stop, I pulled my children back saying, "They aren't going to stop" and I watched as the van rode past me. I saw the name of a church on the side and watched as my next to the youngest son's head came into contact with the front of the van. I immediately began screaming, "God not my baby!!" I remember looking up to heaven and in that moment, I felt God's touch on me. I stopped screaming and began looking around to check on my children. I saw a man coming towards me and I thought he was the driver but God turned me toward the sidewalk where someone had sat my other children down. I realized that they were safe and saw that my son was lying on the ground a few feet from the corner unconscious. When I looked back up, the van was gone and a woman was kneeling over my son, taking his pulse. She assured me that she was a nurse and he was still alive. She told me that someone called the ambulance and people were talking to me. I don't remember everything and everybody but I do remember after the paramedics arrived, I went to the phone booth that was on that corner to call my grandmother and pastor. My grandmother arrived and took the boys to the house to stay with my aunt and then met us later at the hospital. When I called my pastor, I told him what happened and he arrived soon after the paramedics put my son into the ambulance. As I sat in the front seat of the ambulance, I remember hearing my son cry. He was kicking and trying to get up from the gurney. They had put a neck brace on him and ended up having to sedate him. My pastor came to the front of the ambulance and told me that he was following the ambulance to the hospital and that everything was going to be alright. We soon arrived to the hospital and he was taken to the back. I was in a daze, running on automatic. I didn't feel anything and looking back, I know that God continued to keep His hand on me. I remember that as I was filling out paperwork at the counter, my pastor gave me a tissue and was telling me to wipe my eyes and mouth because I had dried saliva and tears. I don't know how long it took for me to be able to see my son or who all ended up in the ER with me but finally, I was able to go to ICU to see my baby. When I walked into the room, his little body was lying in a huge bed, hooked up to all kind of tubes and machines and his head was twice it's normal size. A nurse was standing by him, fixing tubes and adjusting monitors. I looked at him and after a few moments, I turned towards the window and began crying. I was so overwhelmed and finally I let it all out. I don't know how long I stood there but eventually, when I turned around, the nurse looked and said to me that he was doing good. She started explaining that they had to wait for the swelling to go down to be able to see what kind of damage was done to his brain. I went back to his bedside and was thankful that he was still alive. I was at the hospital day after day. He was in an induced coma for about a week. One day when I was sitting in the room, the lunch tray came in. The swelling had gone down considerably. All of a sudden, he sat up and was asking for something to eat! I knew that he was fine because all he did was eat! He woke up and the nurse told me to give him the liquids first. He ate broth and juice for a few days then he began eating solid food. His speech was fine. They had physicians coming in and out and the whole time and he was acting as if everything was fine. He began having physical therapy. They put him on the floor to take his first steps and he was trying to go too fast. We had to slow him down. His steps were a little wobbly but soon after, he was walking fine. His father had come to the hospital a couple of times but I had to stop him because he was arguing with me. I told him I didn't have time to listen to his nonsense. I told him to stay away from me and he did. He was really heavy into drugs by this time. I don't even know where he was staying. I was just trying to make sure my baby was ok. He really made a quick recovery. After two weeks they allowed him to come home. It was summer and he couldn't go outside at first. When he was able to finally go, he had to wear a sunhat to cover the scars. I was so afraid that he would injure himself that he didn't really go anywhere. He played inside but I didn't let him go up and down stairs. If I had to go somewhere and take the other kids, my grandmother would take us. When we went back to church, we were picked up like before and someone would take us back home. By the time school started, my two older ones went back to school and the youngest three were going back to the church's day care center. I had become the kindergarten teacher. I had about 5 students in my classroom and my son was one of them. I didn't really want to teach but during that time, I didn't have anything else to do and my pastor allowed my kids to attend and in exchange for pay I taught. I also bought food to feed the children. I was just passing time away.

I didn't know what I was going to do with my life at the time. I had enrolled in a surgical technician program a year or two before the accident and was doing well. I thought about going into cardiology for a moment. After I saw my son lying in that hospital bed, I realized I didn't have the stomach for it. When I started teaching at the daycare, I enjoyed it so because when I was little, my sisters and I played school all the time. I was always the teacher and because my mom had a massive library, we always had things to read and I would give homework out to my sisters and cousins. But if you asked me what I wanted to be when I grew up, I couldn't tell you and I definitely didn't want to teach! But that is just what God had purposed me to do. I just didn't realize it yet! By the time

October rolled around, I was just existing. I tried looking for another place to live and nothing was working out. My mother had been telling me to come to Texas. I was adamant about not living with her. Family members had gone to visit and they came back talking about how beautiful her house was and how nice it was there. I didn't want any part of Texas! I still had hope for my marriage even though we weren't even together, I didn't want to leave my grandmother even though my aunt and I, who lived in the house, began arguing constantly and I didn't want to leave my church family. I felt stuck and didn't know what direction to take. My grandmother's dining room table was a hiding place for me as a child. After holiday dinners, my sister, cousins and I would get under the table and sneak rolls to eat while the adults were sitting in the living room and we would listen to them laugh and talk about old times. There was a corner in that living room right between the window and the old stereo cabinet that had become my hiding place by this time. I shared the back room with all of my children. We slept on a bunk bed, the three older ones at the top and I slept on the bottom with the youngest two.

I got up early every morning to feed them breakfast and while I was doing my daughters hair, we would sit on the bunkbed watching Animaniacs before school. I was still running on automatic but I was miserable. My aunt couldn't understand why I didn't go to Texas and live with my mom. She even told me that during the arguments we were having. She would say, "You just don't want leave that man, you need to go live with your mother. This is my mother's house. You need to take all them kids and go down there and live with your mother." I know that I was a burden to my grandmother. For years, I thought my aunt hated me. We were close when I first came to live there but that was when I only had one child. She had two boys herself and I guess each time I came back I had another baby so it was a strain of course. I felt alone and helpless. Even though I was surrounded by many, I couldn't talk to anyone about what I was feeling. One night after being up for hours, I went out of my room and went into the dining room in my corner. I sat at the window and began praying. It was dark and everyone was asleep. I was crying and praying inwardly. My soul was tired and I didn't know how much more of the life I was living I could take. I told the Lord I needed help. I stopped crying and in a moment, God spoke to me and said "Go to Texas." I heard his voice, clear as a bell and was taken aback. I didn't want to go to Texas. All of the reasons I had for not wanting to go began to run through my head and I realized that none of them amounted to much. The more I thought about it, the more sense it made but my mind kept trying to say, "but this, but that." Then I heard Him say it again. That night, I finally resolved to go to Texas but it was really God leading me down a path that I never thought I would take. I went back to bed feeling better spiritually than I had in a long time. Now I just needed the courage to talk to my mom and tell my grandmother. I didn't immediately go and start planning to go. Sometime before the accident, I had told my pastor that I felt God was calling me into the ministry. I really believed that God had called me to preach. The first time I told him, he said, "Go back and pray. Ask God if He called you then come back and tell me what he said." I went back a few months later and he told me to do it again. I never went back to talk to him about it afterwards. When I decided to listen to God and go to Texas, I called one of the church mothers and talked to her about what God had instructed me to do. I remember I had taken my son and rode the bus to her house in Jersey City. I called her prior to ask if I could visit because I needed to talk to someone. She told me I was more than welcome and when we got there, she had something to eat. I began telling her that I believed God was telling me to go to Texas. She listened and when I finished telling her how I was feeling she said, "You know I hate to see you go, but if God is telling you to, you have to follow where He leads you." She knew what I was going through with my husband and began telling me about her husband, who had passed. He was an alcoholic and she told me how despite how bad he treated her, she stayed a good wife to him. She told me that God sees me and if I trust Him, He would work it out. I cried while we were talking but she said to me before I left, "No matter where you go, remember that we love you and we are just a phone call away. You are a part of our family. You can always come back to us, you hear me? Don't forget about Refuge Tabernacle." I felt so much peace after our conversation. I knew I had to trust God. There were many times before when I heard him speak and I had to learn to trust Him despite of what I saw around me. So one night I made a call to my mom. I was in that corner and as I talked to her, I began crying. She told me that the reason she built that house was so that me and my children would have a place to live. She said that she was just waiting for me to say yes. She had everything ready. She told me that she would begin making arrangements to come and get me and my children. When I told her that I was ready, a relief overcame me and I knew everything was going to be fine. My grandmother must have heard me and she came into the living room and after I got off the phone she and I began talking. It was late and it was quiet. But there sitting in the dark with the with the street light shining into the window, my grandmother and I talked. I remember her telling me that sometimes, God does things we don't understand and we just have to trust Him. I have always been close to her. She has been my mother just as much as my birth mother has been. That night, although I was afraid of not being near her, I realized that it was time for me to grow up and stand on my own. I had come to depend on my grandmother too much. Every time I got in trouble, I ran to her. Even when my mother was still living with me, I would go upstairs when I got in trouble and in her, I would find comfort. She has become a great source of strength for me but I realized later on that God had to be the one I ran to for comfort, peace, strength and everything else I needed. And so it was, I began preparing for this move. I told my church family. It was hard because I had grown close to them but I knew that it was time to move forward. Outside of my family, I didn't have real close relationships. I had friends growing up in my neighborhood, but I never got really close enough to anyone to be able to be myself with. I didn't have anyone to talk to about what was going on in my life. My sisters and cousins were close to me, but I felt so alone and isolated. So leaving this church where I was beginning to feel like an important part was difficult. My mother made plans to come and get three of my children and drive them back to Texas. I was to come down with my youngest two on a plane. My mother arrived the week of Thanksgiving 1995. She had a truck to take the little belongings we had. People came by to wish me well. My oldest son's grandmother brought him by my house to see us off. She always stayed very close to him whenever she brought him over. He was about 12 years old. I was sad to be leaving but I told him I would stay in touch.

The trip was close to 30 hours by car and my mother had a friend to drive with her. She loaded up my belongings, took my children and headed to Texas the day before Thanksgiving. I was not to leave until December 11. The day we left was somber. I was packed and my grandmother was taking me to the airport. My aunt said her goodbyes but she and I didn't hug. My youngest son was always up under her. He would go into her room to climb into her bed. When he was a baby and we first moved back in, she would hear him at night fussing in his bassinet and before I was up to get him, many times she had already picked him up. I knew she loved me, but our relationship was so strained by the time I left, that I didn't think we would ever reconcile. It's amazing that a few weeks after I arrived to Texas, I got a call from her and we talked for a long time. Over those years, she and I became the closest we have ever been! I realize now that she and I had more in common than I ever knew. She has been through some of the same things that I have been through. She and I often talk about God and the Bible. I am blessed to be able to share with her. Only God can bring about true reconciliation. I thank Him for the connections I have with my family.

When I arrived in the DFW airport in Texas, I was dressed with a heavy coat, a sweater and denim skirt. I saw people dressed in shorts and tank tops. I was floored! The weather was beautiful. The air was clear and there was nothing but land and sky. It was amazing. I was watching the beauty of the prairie as we traveled down the infamous Interstate

35. I remember the kids were talking and my oldest son was reading the signs. He saw Waco on one and was pronouncing it "wacko". We laughed so hard about it. My mother was talking about the schools, the things I could do and what kind of life I could have. I was filled with fear, but I trusted that God would work it out. Finally, after that long drive from Dallas, we arrived in the early evening hours at 405 W. Anderson Avenue in Copperas Cove. I looked at the beautiful 2 story house in amazement as we pulled up in the drive way. The house was on a quiet street with a mountain as a backdrop for the houses. I would later realize there was a creek behind our fence. It was so quiet and serene that I felt a sense of peace. I could feel God's presence in me. The sun was beginning to set and I remember standing on the front porch looking at the sun taking its dip into the western sky. I arrived on a Friday and after resting the next day, I knew Sunday I had to be in church somewhere. My mother told me that there was a church up the street on the corner, so on Sunday morning, I walked up the block to a little church for morning service. It was a small place but I didn't feel a connection. All of the members were nice and invited me to come back but I knew that this was not the place for me. The next week, someone rang the bell and invited me to come to their church. I told them I would think about it. The church was further away from us but I was offered transportation so I took the information and told them I would call. My mother told me about another church that was around the corner. The last time she told me about something around the corner, she said the park. I tried walking my kids to the park one day and we never got there because it was at least 2 miles away. My around the corner was the city around the corner! When she asked that evening after she got home from work did we make it, I told her no. It was too far and the kids got tired. So when she said around the corner there was another church I was skeptic. She told me to just walk down the block and turn at the curve, the church was right across the street. She told me that she thought they had Bible study on Wednesday evenings. So that Wednesday evening, I walked around the corner and sure enough, there was a church across the road. I walked into Unity

Baptist Church and the preacher preached a mighty word. I immediately felt at home! God assured me that this was where I was supposed to be. They didn't give an invitation because I guess it was just regular Bible study but when they were about to dismiss I raised my hand and asked how I could join the church. The people began clapping and praising God and I was ushered in the back of the church with two men and a woman who I sensed their genuine spirits. The woman and I became very close soon after. I would go to her house and she would pray for me during some rough moments that were to come. I told them that I was saved and looking for a church home. I joined that night. They told me to come back on Sunday and gave me the information about service times. I went home that night feeling good about where I was and knew that God was working on my behalf. That next Sunday morning, I got up, got the kids up and dressed and we walked around the corner to church. When we got there, the man who was preaching was not the same man that was preaching on Wednesday night. I would come to find out that this was the pastor. He was preaching even mightier than the first preacher I heard. The choir sang so full of the spirit that I was moved to tears. I knew that this was the place for me. I walked to that church every time they had services dragging my little ones behind me for a few weeks. I didn't stop and talk long. I was just enjoying the services. One Wednesday evening, I was walking down the hill with my children about to go home when the pastor called out to me and asked where I was going. I told him that we lived right around the corner. Just as we had crossed the street and were turning the corner, a car pulled up and one of the ministers that went to the church stopped and told me that Pastor Lewis sent him to take us home. I kept saying it was only up the street and we continued walking. When we came back that next Sunday, Pastor Lewis told me not to walk around that corner anymore. He started making sure we got rides to church and Bible study. I was feeling a closeness with this church and began developing a greater understanding of God. My middle son had begun wearing glasses. He had lost so many pairs, that my mother finally bought him a pair that were made of rubber like the basketball players and they had a band around them. They stayed on and he didn't lose them but when my Pastor saw them, he arrived at my home one day and said, "Sister, I am going to take you to get some glasses for your son." He put all of us in his car and took us to the eye doctor. He got 3 pairs of glasses for $88. He took us back home and told me to let the church know if I ever needed anything.

That is the beginning of what has become 21 years of fellowship with this body believers at the Unity Baptist Church. I have grown so much and so many people have become near and dear to me over the years. There are some who have moved on to other things, but the impact that they have made on my life and my children's lives is still evident. It has not always been easy. I have endured many other trials and tribulations, but my faith has been steadily growing. I can say that my struggles have been a part of making me the woman I am today. I know that the journey I have taken from the moment that I drew my first breath until now has been ordained by God. In my worst moments, He has kept His hand on me. My heartaches are dimmed when I think of God's glorious grace that He continues this day to shower over me and I realize that in Him, I am fearfully and wonderfully made!

Acknowledgements

First giving honor and praise to God, whom, without, I would not be alive and in my right mind today. This journey was ordained before I was born and I am truly grateful that God purposed my path. To my mother, Carolyn Denise Lewis, who instilled in me so much despite her own personal heartaches, I will love you forever and understand why you left when you did. I am grateful that God chose you to be the vessel that brought me into being. Although you have been through hard times, you are still here! Now I want you to "live free" like me! To my grandmother Geraldine Jackson, where my mother couldn't nurture, you took up the slack. You have been my rock, my peace and the one consistency in my life. You have always been a classy lady and I strive to live up to that. Love you much! To my sisters, Chrishele, Adrian and Lea, growing up, we conspired a lot, but you have been my best friends all my life! Even when I didn't know it, you were looking out for me! I love you all! To my uncle Keith, my aunts Karen and Bonnie, thank you for loving on me and teaching me while I grew up. You were all my saving grace during some trying moments and even though it seemed like I wasn't listening, I could always hear you in the back of my mind. To all of my cousins and other relatives, you have all been the fabric that make up the pieces of me! I cherish the memories we have had and love each and every one of you!

To Pastor R.T. Farrell and the former Refuge Tabernacle family in Newark, NJ, I am so blessed to have been a part of this ministry. God has been gracious and I thank Him for the people who were a part of my spiritual growth and development while here. It is here that I learned and saw an example for the meaning of faith! To the memory of Mother's Ada Johnson, Fannie Grimsby, who are no longer with us, and Mother Berneice Zeigler, I thank God for you praying, encouraging and just giving me the wisdom from your own walk with God. Be encouraged and keep working for the master.

To Pastor Richard. S. Lewis, Jr. and Sister Carol Diane Lewis and all the members of the Unity Baptist Church in the city of 5 hills, built for good family living, Copperas Cove, TX, I love you all! It is here that I learned what grace means and I understand my position in Christ! There are some who are still members who have watched this process and countless others whom God has moved to other assignments that are near and dear to me. I thank you and will always keep you in my memory.

To my children, Aaron Wesley Smith, Darryl Troy Griggs Jr., Heather Catrina Griggs, Desirae Maxine Neblett, Travis Brandon Griggs, Jermaine Alexander Griggs and Micheal Ellis Griggs, all I have and still do is for you. You are my gifts. I know that it has not been easy but your love has been the push that has kept me moving forward! When I wanted to give up, all I had to do was think about you and I held on. You are my joys. I would have done things differently if I had known better, but I will never regret bringing you into this world. I pray that one day, we will all be reconciled and spend time together making new memories!

With love,

Sandra

Made in the USA
Columbia, SC
06 December 2024

47576296R00050